TO: D

8/20/15

JOURNEY TO PERSONAL
GREATNESS
MIND, BODY, & SOUL

Enjoy the
read. It was
written with the
passion to help,
people change!

JOURNEY TO PERSONAL
GREATNESS
MIND, BODY, & SOUL

A Blueprint for Life Balance & Self-Mastery

ALVIN BROWN

BROWN BOOKS
PUBLISHING GROUP

Journey to Personal Greatness: Mind, Body, & Soul
A Blueprint for Life Balance & Self-Mastery

Brown Christian Press
16250 Knoll Trail Drive, Suite 205
Dallas, Texas 75248
www.BrownChristianPress.com
(972) 381-0009
A New Era in Publishing™

ISBN 978-1-61254-186-0
LCCN 2015941224

Printed in the United States
10 9 8 7 6 5 4 3 2 1

For more information or to contact the author, please go to
www.JourneyToPersonalGreatness.com

I dedicate this book to those people who believed in me long before I even believed in myself. You all know who you are. Equally, I would also like to dedicate this book to those individuals I've met in life who expressed to me, both directly and indirectly, their reservations about my capabilities. I am not sure how you knew what buttons to push to motivate me, but thank you. Your doubt was a constant source of motivation, and it still is to this day.

Contents

Acknowledgments

I would like to thank a few of the people who have provided the inspiration for and impetus to writing this book. These people have been instrumental in igniting the pilot light and then fanning the fire of creativity that has led to this creation. First, thank you to one of my first mentors and the one who opened my mind to the power of being an insatiable reader, Michael Danks. He has been an influence on me since we met more than a decade ago, and I have never stopped the quest for knowledge and personal development that he instilled in me. Then, there is the influence of another mentor and friend, Dr. Tom Hill. His influence has given me the courage to pursue this project, which is now a finished book.

Thank you, as well, to the fuel for the fire that burns within me, and that's my many friends. They have provided patience, strength, and support throughout the entire writing process. When I think back on my journey that led to this book, my mind always reflects back on this group of people, without whose support none of this would be possible. I included in this group my staff and associates at The Centre for Healing and Peak Performance.

A special thank you to two people who have shown me what is meant by consistent friendship and unconditional support, Virginia Wai Ping and Audra Leslie of Graymatter Marketing Solutions.

Another thank you goes out to Milli Brown and the outstanding group of professionals at Brown Books Publishing Group. You have made my ideas a published reality.

They say that behind every good man is an even better woman, and this is the case with me. I have been fortunate enough to have many great women encourage me throughout my life. Here are just a few: my mama Inez Brandon, my sister Sandra Bryan, my daughter Mohogany Brown, and my mother-in-law Maggie Irvine-Bowles. They always championed me whenever I began to waver and became weak of mind and body.

Then, there are my boys Kami, Delante, and Ebony, always there to teach me, because in them, I see so much of myself. With such a team, losing is not an option!

Finally, there is one person without whom I would only be half a man: my wife, my life partner, my cheerleader, my rock, and my best friend for the past three decades, Suzie Cunliffe-Brown. There aren't enough words to express what you mean to me and how you have affected my life thus far. As my mentor, Dr. Tom Hill, would say, "You married up, Alvin. You married up!" So true.

Introduction

Meet John and Louise Smith. He is thirty-eight years old, and she is thirty-five. They have been married for the past ten years, since leaving college and university, respectively. He studied accounting, and she earned her undergraduate degree in English. They have two kids, ages five and eight, and everything seems to be moving ahead as planned. They have both been consistently employed and working in their respective jobs for about twelve years. They earn a combined annual income of about eighty thousand dollars. Their expenses each month and their desired lifestyle keep things tight, not even leaving enough room for extra savings for their retirement plan. Vacations and other perks are usually by way of credit cards and lines of credit, further extending their debt to equity ratio each year.

Both John and Louise are hardworking and dedicated to living a good life, despite being on life's crowded treadmill, always running but never getting anywhere fast. Since having the kids, they've put on at least fifty pounds between them—John gaining thirty and Louise gaining about twenty. Their energy levels are definitely not what they used to be, and they claim that they lack the time to consistently pay attention to their bodies in a regular workout routine. By their account, they just have enough time to get home and throw some food in the microwave or order out before they have to get the kids to their extracurricular activities. Their days are so jammed with tight and structured routines that it makes each day blend into the next, and before you know it, the weeks become months and the months become years. The problem is who has the time to stop and get off the proverbial treadmill? So even the mention of discovering their passions or going after their dreams leads to a feeling of frustration and being overwhelmed for both of them.

On both mental and emotional levels, the pace of their hectic lifestyle leaves them equally on edge. A seventy-minute commute for Louise and a forty-five minute commuter train ride for John often leave them a bit frazzled before the usual work-related stresses get added on top. Thinking clearly and behaving in a rational manner take massive and concentrated effort, as they are often in reaction mode when responding to any incoming external stimulus, which is usually based in negativity and pessimism. Spiritually, they admit that they find it next to impossible to take time for themselves and connect with a higher level of consciousness. Taking time to nurture their souls through connecting in nature, prayer, yoga, or meditation all sound like good ideas, but, since time is their enemy, this never gets done.

John and Louise are living out of a mediocrity model, which leads to frustration, stress, ill health, and, almost inevitably, a life of quiet desperation. The goal for our couple is to help them shift to a greatness model, one that puts their life back in their hands and empowers them to live proactively and passionately, the way we were supposed to live.

We are all in pursuit of our own personal greatness. As Paulo Coehlo describes in his bestselling book *The Alchemist*, we are all searching for our own *personal legend*. The problem is that we have so many distractions nowadays that it's no wonder we live in frustration trying to even define it. We yearn to be authentic and discover who we really are, and as much as we seem to love having a comfortable level of certainty in our lives, we also need to live on the edge of spontaneity and the excitement of new discoveries as our greatness unfolds. No one is born who desires to have a mediocre existence. Everyone wants to be engaged in a passionate adventure each and every day, only taking some short time away to regroup and map their next course toward their passion.

Life should not be a passive process that we leave 100 percent to chance and hope. Life is about being proactive, disciplined, and focused on the good life. The life you want and desire. Yes, I know, many of us think that life should be spontaneous and unscripted, so we leave it up to chance, just letting the wind take us to some end that we hope is favorable and kind. However, some of us—a small group it seems—realize that life is a game of being proactive and intentional. It's about being vulnerable and brave in order to go after the life you most desire. Many people start out with some sort of a short-term plan, typically up to the age of about twenty-two to twenty-five, which happens to be about the time they graduate from their post-secondary school commitments. Unfortunately, at this point, the dream machine starts coming to a halt, as the only real goal going forward is getting a job in order to pay their accumulating bills and maybe eke out just a bit more to throw in some of the luxuries of life such as the home, the car, and vacations once or twice per year. The other option is that they forgo all the rigmarole of academia and enter the "work force" right out of high school. Either way, the outcome is the same, as both these groups choose to give up their passion in a trade-off for the paycheck or the pension in another thirty to forty years when they can resume the dream of freedom and travel, albeit in a more tamed-down version depending on how they have managed to treat their bodies.

What is amazing is that human beings are naturally goal-seeking organisms, and, before being influenced by the masses, which can collectively include our family, friends, culture, social setting, and so on, we all had a very clear vision of what we wanted, but, over time and through conscious and unconscious programming, we eventually give in and succumb to the influences of the external pressures to conform. We are an average of the people we tend to let influence us on a regular basis. If you look at your finances, your health, your behavior, your consistent emotional reactions, and your consistent and persistent thought patterns, you will start to notice that you are an average of those people you hang out with and you cannot rise any higher and think beyond the walls you have created that imprison you—mind, body, and soul.

We are all in search of our own personal greatness, but mediocrity seems to be our default. That's usually because being and expressing your greatness takes a whole lot of courage and vulnerability and being courageous and vulnerable can often expose you to the big, nine-letter "C" word that so many of us fear: CRITICISM. No one wants to be left out in the open, naked and seemingly alone, to be judged and criticized. What's most impactful about this criticism (and the reason why it hurts so much) is primarily that to be truly great, you must tap into your authenticity, which means that you are tapping into the very core of your being. You have nothing left to hide, and you're completely defenseless from harm. Anyone can now cause you harm, and the pain you feel will be deep and will have repercussions to the level of your soul. It makes sense to want to protect ourselves and step back into mediocrity, take a little off the table, and play a smaller game; that way, when you're hurt by the slings and arrows of criticism, you can buffer the pain by consciously and unconsciously proclaiming that you weren't giving it your all and that wasn't truly your very best.

Taking this kind of position gives us some protection in the short term, but, with consistent retreat to this strategy, the long-term effects are often very insidious and debilitating, as this strategy moves us farther and farther away from our true greatness. Soon you become accustomed to lowering your standards to ones that allow you to be safe from harm, not realizing that this "safety net" comes at a cost. The price is often one that we cannot truly afford to pay back due to the one factor that affects us all, and that's the ticking away of time.

Greatness can be defined as doing anything you're truly passionate about, giving it your utmost effort, and leaving an indelible and lasting mark through your authentic work or art. Greatness means many things to many people. When I refer to greatness, I mean that when you work or play, you are completely engaged and your energy is applied with a focused intention of making whatever you affect that much better when you leave. If you are a housekeeper, gas station attendant, or barista at the local café, then that means being so engaged that when you leave, the space you touched will be filled with your positive energy so that when someone enters your space, they feel as if it was touched by a master. Greatness is when you realize that wherever you go and whatever you touch, it's a representation of the higher level of standards you hold yourself to. It's not about how much you're paid or the ego that is often related to a certain status; it's an internal feeling that you've tapped into the essence of what makes you authentic and what makes you great!

Mediocrity, on the other hand, is all about doing less than your very best each time you're faced with a task that requires you to leave on it your mark of greatness. Mediocrity is about consistently lowering your standards by giving and accepting less than you're worth and less than you deserve. Mediocrity is an insidious process, first beginning as a conscious act that comes from the place of the ego looking to protect itself and eventually becoming an unconscious and habitual act to play small. Mediocrity becomes your default place to go, and you begin to reach for it each time you're faced with a challenge, which is usually associated with an opportunity to grow and evolve into more of your true, authentic self. The bigger the chance for personal growth and evolution to move toward your greatest self, the more the trap of mediocrity works to entangle you in its web.

In this book, you will learn how to achieve your own personal greatness, but not only that; you will learn how to achieve it with a sense of balance and equanimity. There's no use getting the material trappings of life without great health, fulfilling relationships, mental and emotional peace, a sense of connection to your inner being, or high energy levels to last you through the day. What you want is the proverbial cake and to eat it, too. There is no written or hard and fast rule that says you can't have it all! The reason why there are more examples to the contrary is simply that we have all collectively bought into the idea that in order to have abundance in one area of life, you need to take your focus off of some other area that seems equally important, such as your health, family, or relationships. I will admit to you that it will take some focused intention and a clearly defined plan of action, but, with consistent application and dedication to your personal life plan to move from mediocrity to greatness, you will soon realize that you're living the life of your dreams.

The primary focus of this book will be on the integration of the mind, body, and soul and how we can maintain that balance as we move toward our personal greatness. Finding balance is never an easy task, especially in this fast-paced world we live in. Our hectic lifestyles, filled with social media, double-income families, elevated stress levels, and increasing rates of divorce and relationship issues, have caused us to easily go off course and move farther and farther from the peace and clarity we seek. In order to make it even easier to get into the zone of peak performance and to reach your personal greatness, I have broken the mind-body-soul equation into its subcategories and something that can be referred to as your essences, of which there are six: mental, emotional, physical, chemical, material, and spiritual. It becomes much easier to achieve the elusive balance when you can break down the complex triad into the subcategories and therefore put the focus on building and maintaining each.

For over twenty years, I have been on the hunt for practical steps to achieving and maintaining peace and balance in not only my clients' lives but also my own. After working with thousands of clients in many different capacities, I came to the conclusion that the solution and necessary steps to easily apply this information had to be practical and simple. The process could not be filled with cumbersome, difficult, and convoluted steps to get it done. Getting results has to be easily applicable and understandable for you to integrate the changes in your life. If change is going to happen, it must occur from an internal understanding and an identification and connection to your reasons why you should even get up each and every day to build the life you want, to be great!

The fitness, wellness, and self-help industries are multi-billion-dollar industries, and despite the copious amounts of information that are available at various price ranges and on any subject matter, North Americans are still facing an increasing epidemic of obesity and conditions related to lifestyle and diet choices, as well as stress-related issues. This is my motivation to make this information as practical and user-friendly as I can. My approach is to share with you a level of deep understanding and comprehension. I figure that if you know the "why" and "how," you will find the drive to get it done on a consistent basis. This is the key to finally removing the roadblock of resistance you encounter when it comes to committing to move from mediocrity and not only reach but, more importantly, maintain your personal greatness.

I

Defining Mediocrity and Greatness

"Never underestimate the power of dreams and
the influence of the human spirit. We are all the
same in this notion: The potential for greatness
lives within each of us."

—Wilma Rudolph

YOU—yes, you—were meant for more, much more. You were
meant for greatness!

You can never even come close to tapping into your full potential. There's always more in that gas tank of yours. You have a
limitless, undiscovered reservoir of talents and gifts, and you don't
have enough lifetime to discover the uncharted potential that lies
dormant within your soul.

How do I know this when I've never met you or heard your
life story? And what if you are one of those folks who has already
accomplished many great things? Here is what I know, deep within
my soul, and I want to share it with you: our potential as human
beings is an ever-evolving, ever-expanding fountain of possibilities.

Our capabilities are only stifled and stunted by our own choice to accept self-imposed ideas of what we can and cannot be, do, and have. The world at large waits for you to express who you are. Once you believe, we all believe, and the stars and planets begin to align. That's my truth, and that's what I live by!

Before moving forward, we need working definitions of the ideas of mediocrity and greatness. I have to admit that I am the type of person who once thought that everyone should want to be a superstar, to "go big or go home." However, I soon realized that my idea of mediocrity versus greatness isn't everyone's cup of tea.

For some people, a definition of the good life is getting home from work by 4:00 p.m. and watching a couple hours of television or heading out to see friends and socialize. I have to be straight here—that's not my speed. Those who know me know that I am always on, always in creation and dream-building mode.

This is a nice way to say I am a workaholic. There, I admitted it!

For years, I denied this fact although I was the only one I was fooling. I thought it was taboo to admit that you love your profession. I still find it difficult to associate the word "work" with what I do. It feels more like a labor of love, so it's strange to associate it with the same four-letter word other people refer to with such disdain. In the same way, it has been hard for me to believe that not everyone hates to go to bed—after all, sleep just gets in the way—and can't wait to get up and get at it again. I realized early in life that I better love what I do because I am giving up a day of my life to attend to it.

With my youthful exuberance for helping people, combined with a ridiculous level of optimism for anyone's potential to be great, this "I want it more for you than you do" mentality took me quite some time to let go of. I often found myself dragging people kicking and screaming to the proverbial finishing line, which baffled me as to why it was always so difficult with some people. I finally had an epiphany and realized that it wasn't my definition of their greatness that mattered most; it's really about people living their lives on their terms and not just following someone else's definition of greatness.

This issue was a major roadblock for me in the early years because it often clouded my vision to the point where I was unable to effectively guide people to their personal potentials and created a great deal of stress for all involved parties. This is why it is necessary to clearly define what greatness means to someone else—so you can effectively see where mediocrity lies in hiding. One of the first rules for coaching someone is to remember that you should never send your ducks to eagle school. Let ducks be ducks and eagles be eagles. Both will be happy and most effective doing what they were meant to do.

Defining Mediocrity

For me, mediocrity simply means accepting a life that is less than your very best. It's an inner knowledge that somewhere deep inside your soul, you have a space that yearns to be discovered. You just want to be heard for your special gifts and uniqueness. Yet as the days, months, and years fly by, this yearning feels increasingly stifled and muted—not so much by the external world per se but by the host itself—us! What often happens is that each time an opportunity to shine and be heard presents itself, we find ourselves stepping back into mediocrity in order to avoid the slings and arrows of criticism that being vulnerable and expressing your unique gifts can often bring.

This failure to grasp the opportunity to shine could be linked all the way back to a childhood event where we avoided asking to join some group because of the fear of rejection. It could have been refusing to participate in a sporting event or dancing like no one was watching, despite desperately wanting to. Perhaps you told yourself that you weren't good enough or someone else was better than you, all the while feeling that tug from inside urging you to just do it! However, you heard yourself asking, "Why would anyone pick me over them? They are way better than me!" As a final example, there is that memorable and momentous occasion when you were faced with asking that girl or guy, the one you had a crush on, to go on a date or even just hang out with you, but, instead, because of your fear of rejection, you avoided the situation all together. That was a defining moment for you and your spirit: Did you step up and explore your potential or step back into the safety of mediocrity?

These are building blocks that create the foundation for later choices. If we repeatedly prime ourselves to underperform, then it becomes even easier to not ask for that raise, not ask for that promotion, not ask for the sale so you can finally close the big contract or get that deal. How about simply not being vulnerable enough to ask him or her to marry you instead of watching your beloved walk through the door in someone else's arms? This kind of resistance can even show up in simple situations such as failing to tell your partner that you need some time together to connect. These are signs of giving in to the urge to shrink back into mediocrity so you can avoid expressing your inner feelings, which have a deep connection to your true power and greatness.

Living a life of mediocrity is not an overnight event. Instead, it's a subtle and insidious process of lowering your standards in order to avoid shining brightly. This was poignantly written in a poem by author Marianne Williamson called "Our Deepest Fear." She wrote: "Our deepest fear is not that we're inadequate, our deepest fear is that we're powerful beyond measure. It is not our darkness that most frightens us, it is our light." You see, in order to shine our so-called light, we must bare our souls to the world. Being absolutely vulnerable takes tremendous courage.

In today's society, where social media instantly connects everyone, anyone has a chance to voice his or her opinions. While this can be empowering, it can also resemble a weapon in the wrong hands. Anyone can now sit behind a computer and anonymously attack your need and ability to express your greatness and unique gifts. These faceless critics all the while avoid their own chance to grow, expand their level of consciousness, and live out their passion. As the old saying goes, misery loves company, and these people are like crabs in a barrel. Hating to see someone else rise, they pull aspiring individuals back down as they reach for the top.

Simply examine the comments section on any social media application, and you will see the crabs snapping away at the climber who is almost out from the crowd; if that climber becomes tired and beat down from the pull of mediocrity, he or she eventually will fall into the trap of the masses, which is something psychologist Martin E. P. Seligman refers to as *learned helplessness*. This is a limited-belief thinking pattern in which individuals endure adverse experiences, or events in their lives, that are painful and/or otherwise unpleasant, and they eventually become unable or unwilling to avoid subsequent encounters with those events, even if the possibility of freedom exists. These people adopt the attitude that their situation is inescapable and out of their realm of control. This can be a pretty debilitating place to occupy in your mind. You find yourself paralyzed on so many levels: mentally, emotionally, physically, and spiritually.

For the reasons mentioned above, it's essential that we strive to fight off the doldrums of a mediocre existence. We were meant for greatness; we were meant to shine brightly. If this sounds like I'm living in my own Pollyanna world, and you're thinking that I don't know your situation, then I'll just remind you that somewhere in this crowded planet of ours, someone is experiencing far worse than you ever have and, hopefully, ever will experience. Besides, as humans, we have the inherent power to change our course in a millisecond. All it takes is for you to decide and, most importantly, take action.

Other species are driven by their genetic code, which causes them to adhere to an ingrained and automated pattern of behavior. We humans, though, are gifted with a higher consciousness and the ability to choose. So I choose to implement that right and to engage with a more empowering reality. I am urging you and coaching you to do the same.

Defining Greatness

So what is greatness? It means so much for everyone. My take on it is that greatness is simply how you show up in your life. Life is given to us to be filled with passion, but, over time, and for many reasons, we tend to shrink back into a life of certainty and security to avoid the pain of discovering greatness. Greatness is not necessarily about doing something for the sake of getting external attention and approval; instead, greatness is about living your life with a limitless sense of abundance and passion.

Greatness is knowing that you are able to live out your purpose.

If you're a mother, tapping into your greatness can simply mean being passionate about every aspect of being a mom. Get up each morning with a sense of purpose, knowing that you are responsible for instilling the confidence and knowledge that will help your child discover his or her own greatness. If you're a garbage collector, go to your job with a sense of purpose, knowing that how you do the smallest tasks has a profound effect on how you do the big and important tasks in your life. Taking pride in what you do has a profound effect on how you show up in the other areas of your life.

When you decide to go after your greatness in everything you do, you will discover that your life is filled with limitless passion and enthusiasm that will be palpable to all who come in contact with you. You will notice that opportunities come to you in abundance because this kind of energy is infectious and literally everyone wants to feed off your glow.

Moving from mediocrity to your personal greatness is no easy feat, for if it was, all people would have a sense of peace, knowing they have tapped into their greatness and left it all on the table. Instead, I would have to agree with Henry David Thoreau when he said that many people live lives of quiet desperation. Here's the thing: there are many obstacles that can and do prevent us from consistently reaching our best. Notice the word "consistently." Most of us get in touch with our greatness every so often—we have moments of brilliance—but the real goal is to be in your zone of peak performance and optimal living on a consistent basis.

So do you really want to tap into your greatness? (Who doesn't?) Tapping into your greatness is simply your chance to be heard for the individual you are, to be able to express your special and unique gifts to the world. However, the price to get there is what prevents the majority from actually reaching it. Many of us, due to reasons including societal pressures, group influence, fear, and limiting beliefs from past experiences, choose both consciously and unconsciously not to go after our personal greatness. We make these decisions based on a deep, inner knowing that with great power comes great responsibility, and this is where the deep-seated fear rears its ugly head. The thought of it can be overwhelming!

Let me reassure you that this fear can be eradicated with some easy steps: 1) careful assessment; 2) deep introspection to bring the issue to light; 3) journal writing, which is essential; 4) clearly defined plans for consistent action. This is the mind-body-soul journey to discover your light. It was Plato who said, "We can easily forgive a child for being afraid of the dark; the real tragedy of life is when men are afraid of the light." This light he speaks of is a glimpse at your personal greatness, which lies deep within your mind, body, and soul. It's unlimited in its abundance, and the more we tap into it, the more it continues to expand to even greater magnitude.

Here's a little gem for you, a Hindu parable that has been very impactful to me. Sometimes a few words contain such truth that they make you reflect and go into deeper thinking:

> According to an old Hindu legend there was a time when all men and women were gods, but they so abused their divinity that Brahma, the chief god, decided to take it away from men and women and hide it where they would never again find it. Where to hide it became the big question.
>
> When the lesser gods were called in council to consider this question, they said, "We will bury man's divinity deep in the earth." But Brahma said, "No, that will not do, for man will dig deep down into the earth and find it." Then they said, "We will sink his divinity into the deepest ocean." But again Brahma replied, "No, not out there, for man will learn to devise a way to dive into the deepest waters, will search out the ocean bed, and will find it."
>
> Then the lesser gods said, "We will take it to the top of the mountain and there hide it." But again Brahma replied, "No, for man will eventually climb every high mountain on earth. He will be sure some day to find it and take it up again for himself." Then the lesser gods gave up and concluded, "We do not know where to hide it, for

it seems there is no place on earth or in the sea that man will not eventually reach."

Then Brahma said, "Here is what we will do with man's divinity. We will hide it deep down within man himself, for there he will never look!"

Your Action Guide to Discovering Your Greatness

I am a big believer in taking action. I've found that the difference between those who succeed and those who fail really depends on taking right action on the things you know will get you to the life you desire. Too many times, we have great ideas and intuition, but we end up stalling and becoming paralyzed due to indecision and fear. I want this book to be an action guide to help you finally make the changes you need to discover your greatness.

Thinking back, what were some of the key, pivotal moments when you chose to turn away from an opportunity due to fear and uncertainty? Try to recall the story you told yourself about why you couldn't take advantage of this opportunity to grow. Now that time has passed and you are a little wiser, what would you do differently? If you were advising the old you on how to get over your fear, what would you say to help move the old you forward? It's role-playing time now, so I want you to seriously do this! I want you to see yourself advising the younger, apprehensive version of yourself on how great you really are, that the sense of fear and resistance you feel is all in your mind and is backed by nothing substantial. Right now, in this position that you are presently in, you and I both know that the only limitations we have are those that are self-imposed.

Now, step two: I want you to think about a situation you are dealing with in the present moment, one that you are struggling to find the motivation to break through. Would that same advice work for you now? If the answer is yes, then ask yourself: What small action can I take to get it going? Remember: a body in motion stays in motion, and a body at rest tends to stay at rest.

Take action now!

2

Creation of the Mind-Body-Soul Concept

Let me begin by sharing with you a very personal and life-changing story. This particular event was the game changer on how I looked at the clients I was seeing and the integration of the mind and soul within the human body. It was about two years into my career as a manual therapist that I experienced one of my first cases of a real chronic pain sufferer, a woman who had recently suffered a motor vehicle accident that had left her with injuries that were minor but just substantial enough to decrease her overall quality of life. About a year before coming to see me, she had also suffered a loss on mental, emotional, and spiritual levels—she lost her husband to cancer. She described him as her soul mate, and all she wanted, as we all do, was to grow old with her partner. This was taken away from her much too early. After a few months of treatment and many hours of manual therapy that enabled me to adapt to her tissues' feel and tone, I began to notice a level of sensations that I couldn't explain. As she became increasingly depressed and began to open up to me about her steady decline on all levels of her being, her tissues also began to change. They started to lose their natural rhythm and vibrancy. There was an eerie correlation between her state of being and what I felt under my hands.

At first, I denied this connection between what I was feeling and what she was experiencing on psychological, physical, and spiritual levels, but, eventually, it just could not be dismissed. As I worked with other clients, I began to notice subtle but definite sensations underneath my hands as I helped them with a return of health to their bodies. I consistently felt things that were unexplainable to the logical mind. Their different levels of energy, sickness, fatigue, stress, and depression could all be felt as what I can only describe as a high or a low level of vibration and rhythms within the tissues, depending on their overall health. I began to notice that when one of the variables changed (e.g., someone changed what he was feeling on a physical level, or someone had a change that affected her psychology), the clients also had a change in their bodies' rhythms and vibrations! In other words, if you take action to improve your physical body and take the steps to change your thought patterns and/or reduce stress to become better connected with your internal guide, then the vibrations in your body's tissues change.

I had the proverbial "Ah ha!" moment. EVERYTHING is connected.

The Mind-Body-Soul Connection

When we feel prolonged pain of one kind, whether mental, emotional, physical, chemical, financial (material), or even spiritual, we eventually feel pain on all levels: mind, body, and soul. Chronic pain can be debilitating and invasive if left long enough to fester and metastasize into other areas. Pain that initially started in the physical body can have a profound effect on our mental, emotional, physical, chemical, material, and spiritual realities. The same is true for any of the other levels of our being, or essences. All our essences are intertwined, and, like links in a chain, dysfunction of one link, if left damaged and unattended to, can lead to eventual dysfunction of the entire mechanism, leading to an ultimate breakdown.

Believe me; I started where most people begin, believing in only what I could see and what I was told to be the "truth." The typical majority thinking is that the parts are separate from the whole. You are suffering from a weakness either in one or in the other, so the focus tends to be on only one area, the area that screams the loudest in order to find balance. Maybe your weakness lies in your mental game, so you seek counseling? Or maybe a weakness in the area of your physical body, so you seek out tips and strategies to tone and strengthen? Or maybe you've been through some emotional upset and the spirit is depleted, so you head to your place of meditation or worship? The options are numerous, but the point is that we rarely think of taking inventory on all three levels—mind, body, and soul—to see how they interact with each other.

This kind of divided thinking has been installed from the beginnings of modern, organized science and philosophy. Rene Descartes, a French mathematician, philosopher, and physiologist who lived from 1596–1650, wrote in his now-famous thesis "Mind-Body Dualism" that the mind and body are distinct from each other. He argued that the nature of the mind is completely different from that of the body, which therefore makes it possible for one to exist without the other. This kind of thinking has had a profound effect on science, which then trickled down to popular thought on the body and mind over time.

Over the past twenty years, through my life experience and professional practice as an integrated peak performance consultant, I have come to discover that we need to put our attention on the whole person in order to achieve optimal health and tap into our personal greatness. Since mind, body, and soul are intertwined and have a profound effect on each other, trying to check off that goals list, reach levels of peak performance, have better relationships, gain focus and concentration, and achieve inner peace will each become a daunting and weary process if you are not mindful to address and bring balance to this triad.

We truly are spiritual beings having a human experience. I believe the body is simply a vehicle for the soul. It's no wonder that when we age or get sick, it's often our body that ages and gets sick, but our mind and spirit feel timeless and vibrant. And many times, if we allow our spirits and minds to become weak and sick, our bodies soon follow suit. The interconnections are nothing short of amazing.

Due to my skepticism and pragmatic nature (or maybe just my ego not wanting me to look like a flake to those around me), it took me far too long to buy into this concept and embrace it. I kept resisting all the information I studied, all the signs and events that life kept throwing my way, all the while looking for "proof" to explain some of the serendipitous and magical moments I was experiencing in my own life as well as the lives of my clients. I realized over time that there are some things in life that cannot be rationalized by normal means and that defy all logical explanation. It's the mysterious side of life that makes it so magical. The sad thing is that those who don't believe in magic rarely ever experience it.

You don't have to be special or gifted to apply this mind-body-soul concept in your life. The process laid out in this book is completely applicable to deal with our fast-paced lives. I live in the same world as you do—married with four kids that keep us very busy. I am juggling my vision of being a great father and husband while still keeping an eye on my own dream. I realize that the world today is complex and we are trying to juggle as many balls as we can. We all desire to maintain balance in our lives while driving toward what we consider to be of highest importance to our soul's yearning. My own primary goal in life, as I have written and posted on the walls of our healing center, is to help one million people achieve and live optimal lives, and this is what I will do. So let's add your name to the list! I am your coach, and I am here for you.

What you're about to read is a timeline of my personal and professional greatness journey. This is my greatness journey, and I'm 100 percent sure you have one, too. As a matter of fact, everyone does, which is why I suggest that you take the time to do one of these for yourself. When you take this forty-thousand-foot overview of your life's path, you will discover that everything you've experienced plays a part in helping you to discover your greatness. In addition, taking the time to do this exercise will allow you to see how the events and themes within your life are not there to defeat and punish you but are really the universe conspiring on your behalf. You will also discover through your review of your timeline, and with some deep introspection of your life path, that you were indeed meant not for a life of mediocrity but for life at your best and on your terms. We've just spent too much time in denial.

Even the most seemingly tragic experience will have a profoundly deep lesson contained within it. Many times, the bigger your challenges are and the more times you've been knocked down but are able to rise again, the more you are being prepared for ever-loftier levels of greatness. You just have to be able to see life for what it is and certainly not worse than it is. This is the magic of journaling; by writing it on paper, you are able to take a look at your life from a higher vantage point and make rational and unemotional decisions about events you're going through rather than be so embroiled and consumed by them. This is a much better place to be in order to survive your journey.

My Personal Greatness Journey

My goal is to use my experiences to shed some light on your own path to greatness. Within my story, you will be able to see the evolutionary path to the creation of this mind-body-soul idea. You will also see that the concepts within this book are designed based on logical, practical, and usable methods and processes. I know what it's like to start from humble beginnings. I also know what it's like to dig deep and turn it all around through dedication, disciplined study, and clearly defined steps and procedures. I can easily state that I have managed to turn it all around one hundred and eighty degrees, so I could move from my own version of mediocrity to a life that's unlimited and abundant in every way—mind, body, and soul.

Now, even the best-designed plans have snags and will inevitably meet roadblocks, so I invite you to develop a sense of childlike trust for the process. In my case, when I stop to connect the dots on my journey, there is no doubt in my mind that this universe is a series of perfectly choreographed events that are occurring in spite of our inability to understand why, and, if we are fortunate enough to stop resisting and let it happen, what can be manifested and realized is nothing short of amazing! During your journey, there will be magical moments you will experience that are not in the plan, both challenging and great; the deal is that you have to be brave and vulnerable enough to just get out of your own way and trust the process with unlimited faith that God, your Creator, the universe, or whatever you believe in is working on your behalf to make it happen.

Life is unscripted and many times unpredictable, but, if you're open to it, life also has many lessons woven within its numerous ups, downs, twists, and turns that can lead us to our purpose. However, most of us spend so much time in denial of and resistance to our potential that we often cover the path, making it less obvious, therefore losing our way and living life in frustration and despair. I invite you to trace your own story to find the thread that connects each event to who and where you are today. When you start doing this regularly, you will see the consistent theme of your story being played out, which will reveal the path to your personal greatness.

From Humble Beginnings

I grew up in Kingston, Jamaica in the 1960s. My mom, a young single mother, had to provide for five children, so you can easily imagine our constant struggle to maintain the basics of life such as food, clothing, and shelter. We bounced around like nomads, sometimes without a proper bed to sleep on, sometimes sleeping with all five of us kids to one bed. I remember many times we didn't have food to eat, and we went to bed with only water flavored with sugar to give it some taste or condensed milk poured between two slices of white bread. Nutritious? No, but it was something to stave off the hunger pangs. It got so bad for so many days that we used a Jamaican term for it, "air pie and nuthin' chops," which simply meant that we were basically going without for the day.

As bad as things were, though, my family and I made up for it by maintaining strong relationships among us. No matter what happened, we knew we had each other and laughter was always the best medicine. We developed a sense of resiliency and an ability to persevere and find the good points in most of our adversity. I guess you could say that we were abundant in the areas of our mental, emotional, and spiritual essences. Make no mistake; there were some very tough times. Yet, I will always believe that behind every adversity is an even greater seed of opportunity. If you look at the challenges of your own formative years, I believe you will find similar chances you had to learn and grow. It's all in how you choose to make meaning of the events in your life. What I developed from my childhood experiences was a massive level of empathy and curiosity for the human experience, plus a growing resiliency to endure life's numerous challenges.

From a very early age, I have been an introspective person, and through these challenging times, I questioned my life as it was. Why did some people seem to have it all, while others suffered and struggled all their lives? Is it really all about the way the cards were dealt, or is someone able to change his or her present situation to one that is more empowering? Do our past and our cultural up-bringings really determine our destinies? It seemed that everyone around me had a story of how hard it was to get out from the chains that bound them, and when I listened to these stories, it made the mountain of obstacles seem insurmountable. Still, something in me kept saying, "All I know is that I'm not meant to be average."

My mother had a master plan to get out of our situation: we would migrate to Canada and start a new life. There was only one catch; my mother could not afford to bring us all at the same time. Since I was the youngest, I was chosen to journey with my mom to our new home. We landed in a small town just thirty minutes out-side of Toronto, the largest city in Ontario. My mom and I shared a small, eight-by-eight-foot bedroom inside a friend's home. I re-member blue walls, grey carpeting, and a space so small that there was literally only room to walk in and out, lie on the bed, and watch TV. In a way, this was a bonus because we literally had the clothes on our backs and very little in our pockets. Despite our modest surroundings, we had more than enough to start down a new path, and we were extremely grateful.

Actually, I wasn't conscious of our lack of material abundance until I started to hear the other kids take stock of their haul after the Christmas holidays. I became creative and invented a few items so I wouldn't be excluded from the celebration. Being a member of a minority within a new culture filled with new traditions, a different language, and unfamiliar belief systems, I was already an attention-getter, so being inconspicuous was a goal of mine. Although Canada is known for its long history of cultural tolerance, kids were not very understanding of diversity in the mid-1970s. Because my mother worked quite often to make ends meet and save to reunite the family, I spent a great deal of time alone but never lonely.

This period taught me to go deep into contemplation about my life and our situation, and I would not change a thing about it. I developed an amazing imagination, which let me see the future I wanted and who I wanted to be.

Two years passed before my siblings and I were reunited. This was a great moment for me; the family bond and support were back in order. To this day, I am amazed at how my mother accomplished that on a 1970s housekeeper's wages, in addition to paying rent and feeding both of us each day.

Because of this and too many other events to name, I developed the mindset that it's not what happens to you; it's what you do with the situation that counts, as well as your desire to see your dream come to fruition. On the path to your dream, you will meet with a number of obstacles and pitfalls, that is for sure, but if you really desire what you want in life, if it serves the greater good in some way, and if you are willing to make the sacrifice to get it, you will get it done in due time if you just don't quit!

Building Four Essences: Mental, Emotional, Material, and Spiritual

In the early '80s, when I was about fourteen years old, we had to move once again after we were asked to leave our three-bedroom, high-rise apartment. This place was never the greatest—filled with cockroaches, a shoddy exterior, and a constant odor of garbage throughout the hallways. However, it was home for us for about four years until we were too behind on rent and the apartment was being sold out from under us. Our only choice was to move in with my older brother and his wife, in a government-subsidized, two-bedroom apartment in the city. The conditions in this apartment were no better, and the neighborhood left much to be desired.

After a long and deep conversation with my mother, I decided to move out and live with friends back in the small town where I started my adventure in Canada. How would I do it at fourteen years old? No idea! It was simply a matter of trusting in the process and letting the universe do its thing. All I knew was that I didn't want to be average and my present situation was never going to facilitate my growth toward where I knew I should be.

I had to keep my focus on a sense of trust and being able to listen to the universal guidance that is always speaking to all of us. There was an inner knowing that all would be OK. This faith and trust paid off because looking back, what looked like acts of serendipity and luck were really the magic of the universe doing its thing. Many of the circumstances that aligned to get me through that time were just too perfectly choreographed to call it luck. When I step back and reflect on those times, it makes me start to believe in a grand design because there's no way I knew what my next move would be. I reiterate: all I had was a sense of trust in the process. Curiously and ever so timely, certain friends "magically" came to my aid each time I needed it.

During this time, the choreography continued to play out as I met the girl who would eventually become my wife and the mother of our four kids. Meeting her was another pivotal part in my journey. My wife has been instrumental in helping me become who

I am today. Although our early paths were culturally and socially different, both our journeys had their turbulent times, and I think this shared background is the foundation for our thirty years thus far. We've grown together, forged a stronger marriage, and developed strategies for having a great relationship. I have learned that relationships in any fashion, whether personal, business, or social, are key to the process of moving from mediocrity to your personal greatness. You can't do it alone, but whom you choose to take on the ride with you can either make you or break you. Sometimes you can try your best to choose wisely, but each person represents your teacher on that journey. Whether bad or good, it's all part of the design. The process is at work.

A few years later, my mother, the resilient fighter that she is, found us another apartment in a somewhat safer area of Toronto. Although it wasn't high end, it was still a major step in the right direction. We had a roof over our heads and much-needed stability, and this new home allowed me to move back in with the family, regroup, and plan for the future.

Adding the Physical Essence

In my junior year of high school, I discovered the sport of wrestling. Before this, I did not participate in any type of sporting activity, primarily because I lacked the money to pay my own way. Aside from fees for equipment and uniforms, it took very little money to participate in wrestling, and this ended up being a major turning point for me. Being involved in a sport at a competitive level provided a higher vantage point for the path ahead. With each new achievement, and the more I associated with like-minded individuals, I began to see that I could do, be, and have more. This was more than just wrestling—it was a period of personal development and growth at just the right time in my life. The experience gave me direction, passion, commitment, focus, and an appreciation of teamwork, which is necessary if you truly want to do something greater than you can imagine.

This experience was the stepping-stone that led me to other experiences that helped to boost my confidence, as well as instill a feeling of accomplishment and achievement. Eventually, I attained my black belt in martial arts, boxed as an amateur, and danced competitively as well as professionally for many years. With each victory and defeat, I sifted through the noise to reach clarity and find the sweet spot to my peak performance zone. Victory and defeat cause all athletes to take stock of themselves so they can craft their characters. Both martial arts and boxing became more than just channels to express aggression and anger; through them, I developed courage, determination, and a sense of peace within myself to face my fears. I discovered that although each fight came with its own sense of uncertainty and fear, on the other side of fear is a chance to find the foundation of my new strength. Every opponent represented not only a competitor battling for the win but, also and most importantly, another opportunity to discover more of myself on many levels: mentally, emotionally, physically, and spiritually.

Dance also played an important role; dance represented to me a metaphor for the creative process itself, as well as a means to connect with my higher consciousness. Here is what I mean: through dance, I discovered a sense of freedom and liberation as I connected with the rhythms of the music and the choreography. I discovered that dance, like any other art form, is a creative process. Creativity in any sense, through artwork, dance, a piece of music, or writing, follows the same path. What we experience in the physical reality must be first created in the intangible world of our thoughts and emotions. This is the workshop of the idea, and when your feelings of excitement and wonder coincide with your vision, that bubbling well of emotions stirs within your heart and eventually provides the fuel for the creative dream. If you allow yourself to be connected to your higher consciousness and stop denying your greatness, you can easily tap into this abundant and unlimited source of creation.

Discovery of the Chemical Essence

When I was in my mid-thirties, my wife and I experienced a great deal of stress. Each night, we recounted the events of the day, which were all focused primarily on the stresses we experienced. We "vented," which felt like an effective plan in order to blow off a little steam. The effects of our nightly "venting" sessions were insidious, as they became a regular routine. Before we really knew it, we found that instead of relieving the pressure, we were fanning the fire. My wife and I, who were usually mindful of each other's feelings, eventually started to turn on each other. It's funny how that goes, isn't it? When you complain and gripe about anything in your life, the outward effects are not only mental and emotional, but, eventually, you start to feel this negative energy on the level of the soul.

After a few months of these "venting" sessions, and as they gradually began to escalate, I started to notice a gradual loss of pigment in certain areas of my face and body. My eyes, the corners of my mouth, ears, and torso were all being compromised as more and more pigment started to disappear. At first, the changes were slow, but, with the summer sun, I started to notice rapid changes in my skin tone. As I looked in the mirror, I began to wonder, *What is happening to my body, and how far will this go?*

I knew I needed professional consultation, so I made a trip to my doctor. I was informed that I had Vitiligo, the condition that caused Michael Jackson to lose a large percentage of his pigment due to a deficiency of the cells that create melanin, which is responsible for producing our skin color.

I was devastated and taken aback when I heard the news. I couldn't believe that I had developed this rare and incurable condition. After consultation with my dermatologist, I was even more disheartened because I found out that the best the medical profession could do for me was to offer topical cortisone. What was I supposed to do with that if this condition began to affect my entire body? Fill the tub and dive in?

My first reaction, like most people who receive disturbing news, was to enter into the usual pity party, asking why and placing the blame outside myself. This lasted for about a week before I started to look deeper inside myself. I figured that if the medical community was not able to help me, then I must do what I could to help myself. I also figured that since I wasn't born with this condition and no one in my immediate family had it, the only apparent cause was the level of stress I was experiencing, which at that time was greater than I ever imagined. I found out that mental stress, if left long enough, can morph into emotional, physical, and even chemical stresses.

I went on a mission to address this condition head-on! I began a strict regimen of cleansing the liver, getting rid of candida (a type of yeast that can grow in the body), and an overall dietary change. I also increased my exercise program and, most importantly, started to incorporate regular meditation to change my belief and mindset about my situation. After about six months of this program, patches of lost pigmentation began to change and darken, not to mention the fact that I was losing weight and feeling increased energy. It was almost as if I found the fountain of youth. I now had new hope for my condition, and I felt empowered.

This time in my life was the most significant part of my journey. This experience gave me full immersion into my belief of the mind-body-soul interconnection.

Professional Greatness Journey

Like my personal life, my professional journey has been a series of serendipitous moments and times when, after reflection, I realized that I had been led by something bigger than myself. I do believe in magic, which enables me to see it in my life over and over again. Sometimes I may lose focus and start to believe my situation defines me, but, after a simple step away to reflect on the grand design, I am back on track to letting go and trusting the process.

There was a time when, I have to admit, I bought into the prompting and nudging of the crowd, where finding something "safe and secure" for my occupation was my primary aim. It didn't have to be meaningful; it just needed to pay, provide some security, and not be too challenging! Most of the people in my circle shared this goal, so why shouldn't I aim for the same thing? I had done just about anything and everything since I was thirteen years old. When you've lived without for as long as I did, almost anything will do just to have some money in your pocket so you can feel a sense of worth.

Over the years, I did odd jobs such as construction work, picking cherries on a farm, delivering flyers to neighborhood homes, stuffing egg rolls at a Chinese restaurant, working in multiple fast food restaurants, owning and operating a coffee truck, bouncing in a bar and night club, and even cleaning toilets. Was I passionate about any of that? Not really, but I was more passionate about keeping myself from starving and having something for myself so I could feel somewhat empowered as a human being who could contribute to society. You could say that I had an impoverished view of my future and my place in the world. On a superficial level, I felt as if that was the limit of what I had to offer. However, deep within my core, I still knew I wasn't created to be average. Does this sound familiar to you?

I knew deep down I was meant for more, but the problem was that I had no clue as to what it could be or how to even find out. There I was: twenty-three years old, planning to one day get married and have kids, and my dream of a successful career in the martial arts or boxing was looking bleak, even as my goal of making the Canadian Olympic team was getting farther and farther away. Things just weren't panning out as planned. Higher education was not an option, possibly because my current group of friends chose the route—as they announced at high school graduation—of "entering the work force." I thought higher learning was mainly for the privileged few people of color who had affluent parents like the role models from the '80s TV series *The Cosby Show*. Or maybe they were just sellouts who forgot who they were. What I was sure of, though, was that you had to be privileged or Caucasian to go to college. Amazing what you can come to believe if you really want to support your need to stay small, isn't it?

My limiting belief at the time was further reinforced by a few key interactions with people of authority in my academic career and personal life that I allowed to have influence on me. Besides, it just seemed easier not to bother stoking that little ember burning inside. It seemed like a lot of effort, especially when my close friends were all settled on cruise control in their lives, working in their respective jobs and making money. However, that yearning within my soul-space would not be quiet or relent!

Want to talk about being guided? Well, my entire career is composed of moments when I followed the lead and allowed myself to be vulnerable, humble, and trusting enough to listen to the subtle and not-so-subtle messages from my clients, who unconsciously told me through their ailments and intimate conversations what I should study next or bring to the treatments. I was also directed through messages from a higher calling and an inner knowing (or perhaps, for you, God, the universe, your soul-space, or whatever term you may want to use); essentially, it's that message that often starts out as a whisper, and, if ignored for too long, it becomes a constant, unyielding chatter to let you know that you weren't born for mediocrity and your greatness awaits discovery.

So how did I get here? From my start as the youngest of five in Kingston, Jamaica, with a single mother, the odds stacked against us, working my way through all the typical obstacles, speed bumps, and learning lessons that life throws on our paths, to becoming an entrepreneur, achieving two university degrees, being a business owner, and, most importantly, to now having my book in your hand and being able to actually call myself an author? To tell you the truth, I am still amazed by the journey myself. How did I do it all and still be able to honestly say that I am here with all the wheels on—remaining mentally, emotionally, physically, chemically, materially, and spiritually intact, as well as keeping all my relationships healthy and thriving?

Remember: my story is your story, and when you take the time to look at the forty-thousand-foot view of your path, you will see that you have been guided to discover your greatness; you only have to get out of the way!

In order to make it succinct, I am going to give you just a summary of my professional journey in chronological order. You will get a bird's-eye view of the amazingly choreographed path to finding my true passion and personal greatness.

1984

Devry Institute of Technology – Another case of being led by the great design. In this case, I didn't know what else to do, so I followed my brother to the local community college to learn all about digital and analog circuits. After a year and a half, I found out what I didn't want, but, later on, I did notice that analog and digital circuitry works much like the human nervous system … hmmm.

1985 – 1991

Many odd jobs as I set my sights on an easy and secure paycheck. I found myself becoming what Zig Ziglar, author and motivational speaker, often referred to as "a wandering generality instead of a meaningful specific." Once again, I was finding out exactly what I did not want for my future while zeroing in on what I was most passionate about.

1991 – 1993

Personal Training – As my hope for athletic greatness began to dwindle, I realized that I wanted to use that passion to help people live their lives at another level of performance. I figured that the best place to start was at the ground floor—the physical body. My interest in the human body exploded as I scratched the surface and discovered a whole new world that completely consumed my focus and passion!

1992

Therapeutic Touch (Huh?) – While trying to start my career in body work, I stumbled over an energy therapy in what seemed to be, at first blush, a complete error in judgment and a bit of ignorance on my part. However, I later found out that it laid the foundation for my ability to interpret the subtle messages and energies within the body's tissues and to make the mind-body connection.

1992 – 1995

Massage Therapy – Another serendipitous moment along my journey. I later found I was being led and my only job was to listen and follow the clues to my greatness.

1995 – 1999

Holistic Nutritional Consultant – I discovered the importance of the body's healthy chemical balance and how critical it is to your health and wellness. I also learned how subtle signs and symptoms, which are often ignored, can limit our ability to reach our true level of wellness.

1998 – 2006

Manual Osteopathy – Another case of being willing to be led and being mindful enough to get out of my own way. This experience had a profound effect on my belief system and gave me the tools I needed to look at the body from a truly holistic point of view. I earned my diploma in manual osteopathy and later went on to earn a bachelor's degree with honors from the British College of Osteopathy.

2000 – 2008

Acupuncture and Chinese Medicine – I had a strong attraction to this field because of the belief system of the connection between human beings and the earth and its surroundings. Something deep inside me knew this made sense. How could we be separate from our ecosystem? The cures we search for are all around us hidden in nature; all we have to do is search right beneath our own noses and under our own feet.

2005 – 2009

- Psychology – At this point, I needed to connect the mind and body. My clients subconsciously demanded it, so I pursued the necessary knowledge and attained my second bachelor's degree.

- Reiki Therapy – Within this timeframe, I also decided, through the promptings and subtle messages of my clients, to revisit the field of energy and the mind-body-spirit connection.

2006 – present

Neurolinguistic Programming – I became passionate about finding out what makes us do what we do and what strategies each person uses to make decisions. NLP offered me the ability to identify strategies, or in other words, the owner's manual to my clients' decision-making brains and how they view the world.

2007

I took the big leap! I was tired of the idea of treating people from one point of view rather than what I believe is a true holistic fashion. It was time to create a place where I could gather a team of individuals with the aim of treating each client "whole-istically," mind-body-soul. The dream was born, which led to the Centre for Healing and Personal Potential and Integrated Peak Performance.

As you can see, I am a big believer in the idea that where you start in no way forecasts a foregone conclusion as to where you end up. For the sake of brevity, I've left out lots of information and other serendipitous moments that have led me to where I am today. I can easily say that because of all of these incidences, I have developed a sense of wonder and a childlike trust in the process, even if at first I haven't known why something was happening to me.

You can do the same. Even when it may seem like all is lost and your actions appear disjointed and off track, you can develop the ability to step back, reflect on your journey and the events at that time, smile, and return to a trust that all will be OK in the end.

Now, I am not saying to do nothing and just wait for good luck or for your prayers to be answered, but what I am saying is to work with a sense of peace that all will be right in its own due time. You just have to keep the faith and your eyes on the prize.

3

Defining Mind-Body-Soul

Kate was a middle-aged mother of three, married for over eighteen years, who held a secure job with pension due within five years. On the outside, everything seemed perfect, but, deep inside, she knew there was more for her. Don't get me wrong; she loved being a mother of her three amazing kids, and she had done a great job raising them over the past sixteen years, so feeling unfulfilled came with some guilt attached. By all rights, if you measured her life's scorecard against society's prescription for happiness, she should have been very satisfied.

But, like most of us out there, at some point, she realized that time was ticking away and she was no closer to the bull's-eye of her true inner passion. It was in there—in her mind, body, and soul— but the picture was vague and nondescript. She felt she could almost reach out and grab it, but it continued to be just beyond her grasp. After some time, this nagging yearning in her soul started to seep into her entire being. Her physical body was plagued with constant aches and pains she was unable to soothe. Her mind was constantly frustrated by the realization that despite a strong desire to change, the answer remained a mystery.

Kate is not alone in her quest to discover her true self. Many of us get lost in the shuffle of life and caught up in busily being busy. Are we getting anywhere? Are we being productive? Are our actions leading us to an end goal of expressing our authenticity and moving from mediocrity to our personal greatness?

Quieting the Noise

Stop! Yes, just stop for a moment. Try to quiet the noise, even if only for a few seconds—the noise of the daily grind, the worry about the never-ending bills, anxiety about the future—quiet the noise of the ego trying to establish its need to be always right and always in control. Go deep inside to find out your reason for being on this journey. My guess is that, like many of us, you will hear that you are searching for authenticity. To just be heard for what makes you special and unique. In order to quiet the noise and solve the puzzle of finding our authentic self, we must first be able to align our three energies of mind, body, and soul.

The topic of the mind-body connection, particularly the involvement of the soul or spirit, can be a very controversial topic. It is too far out of the belief system and comfort zone for many. So let's clear the air and cover some housekeeping before we move forward.

Philosophers, scientists, and theologians throughout the ages have been unable to reach a common point of agreement as to a definition of the mind-body-soul connection and what it means to us humans as a race. It has been the foundation for many yoga and healing practices for centuries. I think we all intuitively have an inkling that there's something much deeper than our five senses allow us to perceive.

After many years and thousands of clients passing through my treatment and consulting office, it's impossible to deny the correlations and interconnectedness when my clients experience major improvements in their health, as well as positive life shifts due to an integrated approach of treating the mind-body-soul triad. As much as my logical left brain resisted, I eventually stopped doubting the process and started making notes.

I noticed that the triad could be broken down even further into subcategories. We can refer to these subcategories as the essences. I use this term because, just like the literal definition of an *essence* taken from *Merriam-Webster's Dictionary*, an essence is a substance that contains in very strong form the special qualities (such as the taste and smell) of the thing from which it is taken. In other words, the essences are not the true representation of our whole beings but are reflections and components that make up our entire beings. Don't misunderstand, though—the successful balance and harmonization of each individual essence is critical to improving your health and achieving your personal greatness. Basically, getting your six essences in alignment is key to achieving the elusive balance we all seek and yearn for.

Mind

We can separate the mind into two segments, the conscious and subconscious. The brain itself, with its billions of neurons and three-pound mass, can be thought of as the physical and tangible portion that is responsible for sorting and storing our thoughts and feelings, while the mind functions as the intangible but always rich-in-activity and processing-directive portion of the brain. The proper care, control, and guidance of the conscious and subconscious, which constitute this category we call the mind, allow them to work in perfect synchrony and are essential to creating a more empowering reality, helping us move from mediocrity to greatness.

The problem is that most of us don't realize that to have our minds working in our favor takes careful, consistent, and focused actions to train and fine-tune our brains to work for us and not against us. Many people seem to think that we can just leave this brilliant machinery, a brain filled with intricate and precisely calibrated wiring, to merely operate by chance and wishful thinking.

Let's face it; many of us act as if we are wishing and hoping that by some stroke of luck, we will miraculously get the life we most want and desire. I am here to tell you that you can get the life you want, you can be brilliantly successful, and you can achieve your personal greatness, but it will never happen by chance alone. In order to get exactly the life you want, your mind and brain must be actively molded and guided by you, the only director of your life's movie, and not the outside influences of the masses who typically live in conformity and safety. Our minds are constantly bombarded from countless incoming stimuli on a daily basis, through the media, our families, and our social circles. All these incoming messages tend to have an influence on us, affecting our decisions about who we are and what we should be. These push us even further away from our authenticity and back into the proverbial box of conformity.

As much as I love technology, I am keenly aware of the insidious negative effects of social media on our focus, attention, and concentration. As our smartphones buzz, beep, and tweet away, we all instantly react to those notifications so we can get our reward of seeing who has updated their status or how many "likes" we have on the pictures we've posted or the words we've written. It's become a serious epidemic in our society. What was once a novel way of connecting with old friends and family is now a complete addiction and often a place to air our frustrations, dirty laundry, or what we have chosen to eat that night. This technology dependence has us reacting like Pavlov's dogs in the famous experiment where the dog is trained to salivate at the sound of a bell.

Again, I love technology, but when we find that it's robbing us of our focus and attention and inhibiting us from taking action on the necessary steps to achieve our personal greatness, it's time to reclaim our power to manage our time and our reality. Since time is the one commodity that's equal to all of us and one that does not replenish when it's gone, we better learn how to manage it efficiently. With just a few key words on Google, you can come up with a number of studies that have shown that 28 percent of the average office worker's day is spent dealing with distractions and another twenty-three minutes attempting to regain focus. What could we accomplish if we were focused on our goals and fully driven to reach them?

In Bryan Kold and Ian Q. Whishaw's *An Introduction to Brain and Behavior* (2nd edition), the authors state that the conscious mind is the portion of the brain understood to be under our voluntary control. It acts as the gateway to our subconscious mind. We actively choose second by second what is allowed to enter this portion of the mind. The conscious mind is about 10 percent of the function of the entire brain, while the subconscious mind takes up about 90 percent. Neuroscientists have stated that the conscious mind gives human beings the unique ability to function with a higher level of consciousness, allowing us the ability to interact effectively within our environment, create and innovate, dream bigger dreams, and choose our destinies.

The conscious mind, that 10 percent portion of the brain, forms the outer layer of the brain's structure and is called the *neocortex*, or "new bark" in Latin. The neocortex is responsible for higher functions such as language, perception, conscious thoughts, spatial reasoning, and awareness. The conscious mind uses our five senses to bring outside information to the brain so it can decipher the billions of bits of sensory input, delete what's not important at that time, and make sense of the world around us by putting it all into context and order.

According to *The Divided Mind: The Epidemic of Mindbody Disorders* by John E. Sarno, the subconscious mind, on the other hand, is attributed to the lower (in terms of hierarchy and anatomical position) and more internal, or deeper, parts of the brain. It is associated with more "primitive" actions concerning survival and procreation. Functions of this segment of the brain include hunger, reproduction, the fight or flight reaction, emotional responses, and past memories. Some practitioners, such as hypnotists, believe that within the subconscious mind lie old memories from as far back as our childhoods, or even past lives.

Within the more primitive and older region of the brain is housed the *limbic system*. The limbic system contains the processing centers for our memories and emotions. The fact that it is more established than our neocortex, or a more recently developed portion of our brain's anatomy, means that it becomes that much easier to conjure up memories and emotional reactions to events and circumstances in our lives. This simply means that if your desire is to live a life of peace and harmony and to reach your own definition of greatness, it is essential to train your brain to have control of this key area, which can be done with focused intention and repeated practice. We will go over these practices in much detail in future chapters.

Body

I went to lunch recently with my family in a busy downtown metropolitan area of Toronto. As I waited for my family to arrive, I started to people watch. I love doing this—just observing people as they wander through the world lost in thoughts and conversations and watching the great variety of people around me, appreciating the great diversity of folks. For some reason, my thoughts began to wander, and I began to think about the real function of our physical body in this life experience. Is the role of the body simply to fill out a pair of jeans or maybe provide something to drape a nice shirt or dress on? Is it meant to be ignored and abused, as most of us tend to do, only paid attention to when it's broken?

As I looked at the various shapes and sizes of the people walking by busily on their different personal journeys, I pondered the fact that inside the shell called our bodies, or, as I heard them referred to, our meat suits—no matter how bent, stooped, crooked, or diseased the containers may be—deep within us are housed all our feelings, emotions, dreams, passions, and desires. Externally, the body may seem ravaged by time or dysfunctions or disease, and the contents within the container—which include the organs, intestines, and a myriad of roadways of the circulatory system—may have also experienced the abuse of our habits; still, the deeper, intangible part of ourselves, the spirit, remains timeless and pure, immune to the external world's barrage of potential enemies looking to mar the body's innate and original beauty.

Within the body and its tissues are all our history and past experiences. Many times, in my practice, I have viewed my client as a massive historical anthology filled with volumes and volumes of stories waiting to be read. If only we could read the tissues' vibrations for their historical content, they would tell such stories of pain, turmoil, personal stresses, and triumphs. The body is a bridge between the physical and soul, or spirit, realities.

The body can be thought of as a storehouse for the mind and the soul. After many years of practical, hands-on experience with thousands of clients, as well as a ridiculous amount of research on the human mind, body, and spirit, I fully believe that we are literally spiritual beings having a human journey. It's not too hard to get to this level of belief. Consider that in our minds, on a daily basis, we often live a completely separate experience than the one we actually live in the natural, physical world. If you were to ask ten different people about the same experience, you would get ten different answers. The physical body remains constant in the physical plane, but, all the while, inside us, there's an internal barrage of feedback and processes at work in order to maintain a stable internal environment so we can manipulate the physical world. Whew!

Here's what I am getting at: inside of you, there's a voice, a voice that reasons, introspects, contemplates, makes goals, and looks forward to the future (or maybe even fears it?). The mind is timeless, which is why our chronological age may be eighty years old, but, barring certain diseases of the physical brain, we remain young at heart. So the physical body may suffer the ravages of time, but, inside, there is a vibrant, youthful, and timeless you. As a matter of fact, most of our true aging begins inside with our thoughts and feelings about our reality.

Think about our nervous system, muscular system, endocrine system, immune system, reproductive system, and so on. These systems, working as a unit, are all functioning toward one goal: to maintain and perpetuate life. I am going to ask you to take the position of a research scientist trained to look at things from a place of objectivity, to remove all the emotional and philosophical parts of their experiment and remain as pragmatic and neutral as possible. If we take this stance when considering the functions of the human body, we will see that all the various systems within our bodies were built to allow the survival of the human species. But, if we were to extend this thought and include the entire ecosystem, the trees, animals, flora and fauna, and our place within it, we will then see that in reality, we were made to be perfectly whole to not only survive but also thrive. If we were to be truly in tune with the environment around us and would listen to the signals coming from our bodies, combined with advances in modern medical technology, human beings would not only have increased quantity of life, but we would also have an amazing amount of quality as well.

The Nervous System

The nervous system not only monitors our bodily sensations and sends feedback to the central computer—the brain—but it also scans the external environment for threats that may cause us harm. Once the nervous system receives incoming information, it begins a series of processes aimed at maintaining homeostasis, or balance, within the body. The nervous system has connections with every other system in the body and can launch an attack or send information in an instant!

The nervous system is separated into two types, one voluntary (the somatic nervous system) and the other involuntary (the autonomic nervous system). Both continuously monitor and maintain an internal check and balance system. The great designer and engineer already made account for our numerous weaknesses and distractions as human beings and did not leave 100 percent of the vital processes to us. We were given the ability to manipulate our environment and react to immediate events that may pose some danger to us, but the day-to-day inner workings such as control and monitoring of a perfect and balanced internal environment were left to our automatic mechanisms.

The Muscular System

The healthy and functional muscular system allows us to manipulate the physical world around us and gives us beautiful and graceful movements. With signals from the brain to express to the body all our impulses and desires, the muscular system, aided by the nervous system, elegantly performs a series of intricate movements in order to get the desired request completed. We walk, run, dance, and compete for survival and our future mates, all through the power of our fully-functioning muscular systems.

The Endocrine, Immune, and Reproductive Systems

The endocrine, immune, and reproductive systems all function in synchrony to ultimately maintain balance within the body and carry out the acts of elimination and procreation. When you think about the amount of activity that goes on in the background on a daily basis in order for us to simply enjoy life, you should be amazed and grateful that you've made it this far without fail. Right now, as you're reading this information, your body is launching an attack on some virus or bacteria trying to wreak havoc in your body. Right now, in this moment, your body is filtering, repairing, and balancing a plethora of hormones and byproducts of regular metabolism, all without your conscious input.

In closing, let's summarize all that was touched on into a few paragraphs. We often take it for granted, but our bodies are simply amazing. They allow the soul or spirit to reside and express itself. The body permits us to survive the constant barrage of seen and unseen enemies that are aimed at our eventual breakdowns. Our ongoing task is to slow the process as much as possible, to tip the balance to our side. The way to do this is to be mindful of getting out of our own ways, stopping the frequent and voluntary self-abuse of stress, worry, or improper dieting and lifestyle habits, and instead giving the body what it needs to do what it does best. Not only would we live longer lives, but our overall quality of life would also improve tremendously.

The diseases we suffer from in today's society are mostly "auto-immune," which describes a state where the body begins to attack itself due to erroneous incoming messages. This is usually perpetuated by a bombardment of incoming stresses from the outside that fight against the body's own internal processes. Constant exposure to this external onslaught causes turmoil inside the body and reduces the optimal function of all our protective and life-promoting systems. Simple activities such walking outside, meditation, journaling, and connecting to nature are all good remedies to mitigating this abuse.

There's no use dreaming and wishing for personal greatness when the physical body isn't capable of fulfilling its role. Will eating right and maintaining a physical regimen to build your body guarantee great health? This is always the underlying question offered by those willing to settle for less than their best. I look at it this way—as my long-time mentor, Dr. Tom Hill, said, "You simply want to put the odds in your favor." By doing that, you know you've done your part by providing the body with the resources it needs to function at optimal and peak performance levels. In future chapters, I will provide you with the tips and strategies to give your body the tools it needs to recapture and then surpass your personal best.

Soul

The word "soul" can mean so much to so many people in so many different cultures. The word connotes a sacred place in us that signifies a higher level of being. If certain music is said to move us, it's often because that certain piece touches our souls. When we feel something on a deep level, we tend to say we feel it deep in our souls. The soul is often thought to reside somewhere in the chest in and around the heart space, which implies that this word signifies something near and dear to our hearts. The soul can be thought of as ethereal in nature, something above and beyond the average earthly and material concerns we tend to struggle with. In order to maximize the level of the soul, we must rise to another level of self-actualization.

When people connect at the deepest level, they are said to be connected at the level of the soul. This is true connection, hence the often overused term "soul mate," which can be thought of as your one true and lasting love. A kind of love that can never be extinguished by ordinary means. This is no ordinary love; this is the love that only comes your way once in a lifetime, and only a gifted few will have the privilege to connect on this deepest level.

In the context of this book, when you are able to connect on the level of the soul, you will be able to connect with your greatness because this is where your creativity lies. This is the area of your true self, your authenticity. Artists, musicians, athletes, actors, or anyone looking to tap into their deepest and greatest self must be able to access the soul. This is why many of these creative types who desire another level of creativity will go about it through mind-altering drugs that allow them to transcend the negative reality we struggle with on our day-to-day journey. We often need to knock out the conscious mind with its constant chatter and negative barrage of limiting beliefs from past hurts in order to get to the level of the soul, and ultimately to our true creative genius.

We could never discuss the topic of getting to greatness without considering the repair and nurturing of the soul. That would be like building the tallest building on a weak and shallow foundation. Once we are able to tap into our soul-spaces and mine them for their multitude of treasures, our potentials become unlimited and our abilities to reach beyond our perceived limitations become a perpetual and automatic act that we perform each day of our lives.

Mastering the Triad of Mind-Body-Soul

I predict that you likely fall into one of a few categories. Maybe you've built your finances and professional life to become secure and at ease on a monetary level. Or maybe you've invested most of your time in your family and social life so that you've built up a secure foundation of social support. Or, like many of my clients in the fitness industry, perhaps you've invested an inordinate amount of time into your body, and you've carved your body to look like Adonis. You may even be the type who has disciplined yourself to have two or even three of the above in perfect alignment. However, you still find that you struggle to achieve true balance and to finally break through to your greatest self, to tap into your true personal potential. The question is, How do you realistically achieve the quest to be your best?

In order to achieve balance and harmony in our lives, it's essential that we effectively manage the mind, the body, and the soul. There has to be a perfect level of balance; excess in one area will lead to a diminution of the others. Not enough care and attention to one area, and you can be sure that there will be an eventual overabundance in the others, leading to breakdown. Perfect balance and harmony is the primary goal. However, as we all know, this is not as easy as it sounds, especially in today's society, where we are consumed by the constant distractions of technological advancements and our hectic lifestyles, where every beep, tweet, and ring demands our attention, meaning we lose another grip on our ability to stay focused on what we really want in our lives and what really matters most. As we drive, walk, and socialize, we now find our heads and our attention faced downward staring into a handheld device. Most of us today find it easier to text someone than to connect on a personal and physical level. The art of connecting with others and, most importantly, ourselves, is becoming a lost art.

What we need is an easy, practical, and applicable method to recover this degradation of our authenticity and sense of self. What I'm going to do next is to break down the mind, body, and soul triad into its subcategories, which I refer to as its essences. To review, there are six: mental and emotional (belonging to the mind), physical and chemical (belonging to the body), and material and spiritual (belonging to the soul). This is the model we'll be working from as we progress through this book. The goal here is to break a complex subject into bite-sized chunks so you can apply this information to your life right now.

Remember Kate from the start of this chapter? We worked together to balance her six essences, and she went on to become an entrepreneur, discovering that she had an aptitude for helping other women get out from under their own mountain of conformity and live their best lives. She had a hidden passion for operating her own personal training and lifestyle studio. She had been sitting on this idea for ages, always afraid of taking a chance to break out and just do it. When she mentioned her dream to those close to her, they would look at her as if she had gone mad. These were the pivotal moments when she decided to step back into mediocrity. She basically traded her passion for a pension.

There's nothing wrong with this decision to be safe and provide some security for yourself and your family. Taking chances and pushing your comfort zone is not for everyone. Yet, if you find that the pain of staying the same outweighs the chance you'll have to take to reach your goal of feeling a sense of significance, personal growth, contribution to the world, and fulfillment, then my advice is that you start making your own plans to move toward your greatness. Life is much too short to settle and die with your music still in you.

Kate's business continues to grow each year, and when you meet her, the energy and passion that she exudes is palpable, particularly compared to the feeling you would get when you met her in the past—that something was missing, that her energy felt depleted. In contrast, she now glows with a sense of unlimited potential, and her outlook for the future is not one of fear and apprehension but one of personal power and optimism. She turned her story around.

You can do the same thing. Let's get started.

Mind

4

Mental Essence

"The destruction of mediocrity is one of the most precious of life's pursuits."

—Robin Sharma

You jolt awake out of deep sleep. It's the middle of the night, hours before your morning alarm. The room is pitch black and utterly silent. You toss and turn, thinking, *I've got to get back to sleep. I can't afford to lose this precious time.* Your alarm will be going off in a few hours. However, it isn't long before the mental wheels churn away, flipping through a thousand scenarios as you relive the past and look further into the future. This would all be well and good, except that most of the movies we create in our heads are mostly negative in nature. With this incessant mind chatter, you are now fully awake. The thoughts have triggered a physical response in your body. The more you attempt to shift your focus and think about getting back to sleep, the more the mind seems to be like an unruly child who's in the midst of a full-on temper tantrum, kicking and screaming in protest.

Does this story sound familiar to you? This scenario is just one example of the mind's power in dictating and guiding our reality. Even greater problems result when, in our waking moments, we leave our minds unchecked and running without control and guidance.

British philosopher, writer, and social critic Bertrand Russell said, "Many people would rather die than think!" Here's the deal; most of our habitual thinking is fixated on the negative side of life—what we didn't do right that day, last month, last year, and so on. We can also catch ourselves ruminating on those we feel have offended us and how we're going to find a way to make them acknowledge our feelings. I could probably go on and on about the myriad of self-defeating thoughts that roam through our heads on a daily basis. The general consensus is that we humans think and process about fifty to seventy thousand thoughts per day. According to John E. Sarno in his book *The Divided Mind*, the problem is that most of them are steeped in negativity, so we're beating ourselves up all day long. The subconscious mind is timeless, which means we have the ability to relive experiences and their associated feelings as if they happened yesterday or are even happening right now. When we let our minds ruminate about a time in the past when we felt disappointment, sadness, or shame, the feelings that come with those thoughts are often so strong that they cause us to feel as if we are living in the present moment.

Why do we have such an affinity for negativity? The best explanation I've heard is that this is a built-in survival mechanism. Our ancestors, who were constantly exposed to the dangers of a wild and unpredictable environment, would not be wise to charge through their surroundings without any regard for the possible impending dangers. Their senses had to be heightened as they constantly looked and listened for danger, and they had to assume the worst. They also had to have strong emotional memory about an event so they could recall it in order to help guide their future decisions. That rustling bush didn't mean they should wander over and peer behind it; that strange noise in the distance did not always mean to investigate. Millions of years ago, if we were to survive, our awareness and thought processes had to be constantly tuned in for dangerous predators, and although we now have less need for such sensitivity to potential hazards, we carry our old programming into the future with us and will often use it against ourselves.

Because we are inclined to entertain negative thinking patterns, we should avoid the mistake of believing that all mental processing constitutes a productive form of thinking. When I describe the process of thinking, I am discussing thoughts that are self-directed and growth promoting. Effective thoughts move us forward to the life we most want and desire; these are thoughts that eventually serve the greater good, solve problems, cure diseases, create peace, or help humanity in some other way. There must be some useful end to our daily pattern of thinking, rather than regurgitating old and useless information that only serves to bring us down and make us feel less than our greatest selves. Other animals are driven by their genetic code and must often function by rote through ingrained programming. We humans have a choice on how to think. In every moment, we have the potential to change our directions and our behaviors. We can instantly tear up an old script that doesn't work for us and create a whole new one—we just have to want to change.

Activating the mental essence is about developing a sense of control over your conscious mind. The conscious mind can be considered the gateway to your thoughts, feelings, and emotions. The thoughts we consistently allow to inhabit the conscious mind are the same thoughts that are stored in the subconscious mind and eventually become our habitual thinking patterns. If those thoughts are ones that do not push you to reach your personal greatness, you will find that you move farther and farther away from your most desired life.

Every thought eventually leads to some kind of physical action and reaction. Negative thoughts that are allowed to linger and persist in the subconscious mind will eventually have a profound effect on the body's physiology, causing a host of mysterious and destructive physical complaints. This once again supports the intimate interconnectedness of the mind and body. This reminds me of a client who told me of an intractable skin condition he had as a child. It was relentless and continued to worsen as time went on. All the medical experts were baffled by his symptoms: oozing sores all over his body, with red and flaky skin surrounding each wound, which seemed to continuously spread over his body as time went on. In medical terms, they referred to his condition as *idiopathic*, which is defined in *Merriam-Webster's Dictionary* as any disease or condition that comes about spontaneously or for which the cause is unknown. There seemed to be no explanation for his disorder.

Eventually, a friend suggested that he make a visit to a hypnotist that he'd heard about who seemed to have an answer for some of the strangest health conditions. At first, my client's reaction was to push back at the suggestion, but, at this point, what did he have to lose? The conventional medical route had seemed to fail him so far. Upon his first visit, he was asked the usual battery of health-related questions, but it was not until an inquiry about his family history, when he revealed that his mother was going through chemotherapy and radiation, that a hint about the source of his strange skin issue came to light. They found out that he developed his skin condition sometime after his mother developed similar sores and blisters on her skin caused by radiation to treat her cancer, and since he was intimately connected to his mother on emotional and spiritual levels, he started to manifest her symptoms! This theory was also supported when, after two sessions of hypnosis, his skin condition started to spontaneously improve. It would eventually heal completely. The condition they found was related to a deep-seated emotional release through the largest organ of elimination we have … our skin. You can never deny the power of the human body to find outlets to rid itself of pent-up blockages within each of its essences.

The good news for all of us, though, is that human beings are amazing creations, and with just a little effort and focus, we can change our lives and our health in an instant. However, although change can be instantaneous, it still constitutes a choice. You must want to and be open to change. No matter what has happened to you in the past, you must realize that you have a strong influence on how you choose to live out your future. Don't get stuck in thinking you've tried it all and all is lost. The mind, body, and soul are always working in your favor, but you must be open to searching. The answer will soon be revealed. Matthew 7:7 says, "Ask and it will be given to you; seek and you will find; knock and the door will be opened to you." These are very powerful words to live by.

In this chapter, we will look deeper into the reasons why we form such negative thinking patterns and how we can change them. As the old and often quoted saying goes: If you give someone a fish, he may eat for today, but, if you can teach someone how to fish and get his own meal, he will ultimately eat forever. That is the goal for me, to show you the basis of how we get off track in our thinking patterns, heading toward a direction that seems to perpetuate even more stress and frustration instead of the peace and liberation that we all yearn for. The freedom we search for lies between our ears.

Habitual Mental Thinking Patterns

Picture an expansive field of green. As far as your eyes can see, there's nothing but acres of lush, green, and grassy earth. Then, out of the untouched emptiness of green, you notice a little man beginning to make his way through the tall, thick grass as he attempts to cross the field. He has difficulty making it through—he's a little bit clumsy, and everything he tries seems awkward and frustrating because this is a road less traveled and a new path needs to be taken. However, he's determined, and he doesn't give up easily; he repeats the process the next day. This time, his journey seems a little easier.

After about a week, you come back to see how he's progressing. You notice that the path he forged is now well worn and quite visible among the mass of greenery. Crossing the field is much easier with this path, and it almost seems effortless compared to his first crossing.

After a few more weeks have passed, you check in again, and now you notice that he's found a new direction. His original path is no longer clearly demarcated; the groove begins to fill in again due to lack of usage. As the weeks go by and the activity on this path reduces even more, less and less of the route begins to show. The man forges new routes to cross the field, and getting through to the other side looks as difficult as it was when he first started down this new and uncharted path.

This metaphor is a great way to describe what happens to the brain once you begin with a new task and create a new habit. When you first begin any new activity, it will seem cumbersome, awkward, and totally out of rhythm, but, with repeated attempts at the same activity, you begin to carve a clearly demarcated pathway in the brain, which makes it easier to fire the impulses needed to do the activity with less effort and energy. This process is called *sensitization of the nervous system*, and this is the same process taken by true professionals and experts in any field of endeavor. These people stick to something and do it over and over again, building the pathways to wire that activity into the nervous system so they can build the coordination and firing pattern needed to make the activity look effortless and unconscious. It's the old saying that "Practice makes perfect." Some people even add that "Perfect practice makes perfect."

On the flip side of gaining expertise in a desired activity, this process also applies to habits that don't serve us well. Many times, we are unconsciously oblivious to the neural pathway we are building up due to constant repetition of a habit. Often, these habits are patterns that don't encourage growth but, instead, keep us in mediocrity and frustration. After many repeated actions, this certain habit that began as a conscious act eventually becomes unconscious, which makes it that much easier to fire that grooved and ingrained action to the point that it becomes our "knee-jerk" reaction to any stimulus that causes it to fire (most frequently when we're under pressure or stress). It could be a look, a smell, or just the sight of a certain stimulus, and you are now reacting, or even overreacting, to a slight provocation. You didn't mean to lose your cool at your coworker, but something about how he said that phrase triggered something in you. You've tried to quit so many times, but, when you're around those certain friends and that specific environment, you just can't help but have a drink and a smoke. Because habits are formed on many levels—mental, physiological, and chemical— quitting anything will seem impossible and takes great effort to get done.

For many people, the struggles in their lives aren't related to certain habits but are more related to their thoughts about their situation. Human beings need and want to have options in life. It's when we perceive that we have only one option to any situation that we start to create mental roadblocks and frustrations. Let me elaborate on this point: What is your natural reaction to people who push your buttons or seem like they're taking advantage of you? Is it to react in an aggressive and confrontational style in order to protect your ego from getting abused? Maybe in the past you've been picked on or taken advantage of, and you've now vowed that you'll never let that happen to you again, so you have chosen to react in a manner that is swift, firm, and direct. Maybe you've gone the opposite way, and you've chosen to retreat into a shell in order to avoid the situation altogether. The same questions apply when you face any situation in life—your finances, relationships, professional life, or whatever area you struggle with—the questions are these: How do you react? Does your reaction cause you to grow toward your greatest self, or does it cause you to feel even worse after the event has passed? Do you feel like you mastered that situation, or did the situation master you?

The goal of having balance in your mental essence is to realize that you have a myriad of options for how to react in any situation. It all depends on the outcome you desire from that certain scenario. Richard Bandler, one of the founders of neurolinguistic programming, wrote, "the meaning of communication is the response you get," which simply lets us know that if we don't get the correct response to our communication, then we have the option of changing how we express ourselves until the desired response has been gained from the person we're communicating with. When we become frustrated in effectively communicating and negotiating with someone, it's usually because we fail to exercise our options to choose the words we use to communicate in order to get the right response. Great communicators realize that if they don't get the response they want, they have an option to change what they say until they do.

Many times, our knee-jerk reaction depends on the grooves we've patterned in our nervous system and the memories we've stored in our subconscious, which help to create the stories we tell ourselves. These grooves, memories, and stories become the framework to our automatic way of reacting. If you find yourself reacting in this instinctive way, it is an indication that you've patterned yourself to believe that you have only one option to a certain situation, even when that reaction doesn't serve you. You will also know that you've narrowed your options when you have a deep feeling inside that you should behave in another way—calmer, cooler, and more collected—but you just can't seem to get control, and the situation goes careening off the track. By the time it's all over, you're once again either in an uncontrolled rage or agreeing to some situation that completely goes against your better judgment or moral values. It's time to do something about it!

I believe we create our world around us. Whether "bad" or "good," we are always in creation mode. Yes, life is unscripted, and things happen to us that are often out of our control. But how you perceive and react to your situation makes all the difference. For example, a big financial loss may cause one person to feel like a failure and go into deep depression, while another person can look at the same situation to find out where things went wrong and how to avoid the same scenario if it ever happens again. And believe me; it most likely will happen again. That is life. We are bound to repeat the situation if we aren't able to learn and grow because of it. However, when we get mired in our situation and become consumed by it, we cut off our ability to see the lesson within the circumstances that occurred, and, therefore, we are certain to repeat our mistakes in the future.

What if someone you care about passes away? Death is never easy to deal with, but, again, it's all how we process the event and how we choose to label it. In one scenario, one person may focus on the loss of a loved one and the fact that they will never be together again in this life, while the other person may focus on the fact that life is unpredictable and short at best, build a practice of savoring each moment in life, and tell those that are close to her that she loves them each and every day. These types of people are vulnerable enough to say, "I love you," in addition to taking the time to appreciate those around them. When we choose to focus on loss, especially the loss of someone we love, we get stuck on all levels: mental, emotional, and spiritual. When we get stuck, we once again lose our other options, which creates mental and emotional stress and tension. When we are open to embrace and allow ourselves to process any event to its end, we are more likely to ease the impact of any event and facilitate our ability to get through it successfully.

Let me remind you of the story of Dick and Rick Hoyt. Rick was born with the umbilical cord wrapped around his neck, cutting off oxygen to his brain. This loss of oxygen to his brain during the birth process caused Rick to develop cerebral palsy. The doctors at the time suggested that Dick and his wife institutionalize their son Rick, but the Hoyts made a promise that Rick would live a life that was as fulfilling as possible. During a college basketball game years later, Rick heard his calling as the event organizers announced a benefit run for a cross-country runner who had become paralyzed in an accident. Rick felt the need to give back and asked his dad if they could do something to show that life isn't over because you're paralyzed. This request in 1979 was the impetus to begin their legendary legacy of marathons, triathlons, and ironman competitions. This father and son team—featured on Oprah and discussed on numerous Internet sources—has now run over thirty Boston Marathons and 1,091 races, with the goal of raising awareness of cerebral palsy. It's all how we react to any situation and use it to create a beneficial outcome.

You Can Change

Not too long ago, it was commonly believed that once your brain was wired a certain way, that was it—there was no going back. It's the old saying that "You can't teach an old dog new tricks." However, research has shown that not only is change possible, but it's a constant and our brain and nervous system are always being affected by our environment and life experiences. Every new event or experience has a profound effect on our entire structural wiring. Constantly pruning away and building new tracks enables us to learn, grow, and adapt throughout our lifetimes. This process of adaptation and change in the brain due to external and internal stimuli is known as *neuroplasticity*, which explains how the brain is subject to change due to both good and not-so-good events in our lives. The more we are exposed to any stimulus, the more the nervous system becomes sensitized, allowing faster and more efficient firing and reactions to the same event or experience. It has been extensively researched that constant exposure to stress (mental or physical) causes significant changes in the brain's tissue, remodeling the brain and making it that much easier to become prone to feeling stressed over most challenges we may face.

Neuroplasticity explains why it takes anywhere from thirty to sixty days to install a new habit. The efficient integration of any new habit needs that time to allow the nervous system to become fine-tuned, automatic, and coordinated. If the ideal amount of time isn't given to learning and incorporating a new habit through constant repetition, then the appropriate nervous pathways will not be laid down, and, therefore, no permanent, significant change will take place. This goes back to the four stages of learning any new skill, attributed to Noel Burch of Gordon Training International in the 1970s.

The theory simply states that we learn through four stages: *unconscious incompetence*, where we do not know how to do something and cannot recognize that we are deficient of this skill; *conscious incompetence*, where we are aware of our inability to perform a certain skill but are still unsure of how to do it; *conscious competence*, where we are completely aware of both our weakness and how to correct it, but it requires all our attention and focus to get it done; and *unconscious competence*, where we are completely fluid and versed at performing the skill without focused attention and energy. At this last stage, the acquired skill becomes effortless. We can attribute the transition through the four stages of learning to the repeated practice and exposure to the new habit, along with the fine-tuning of the nervous system that results. Professional athletes practice on a daily basis, often hours per day, in order to achieve the fourth level of learning. This can be referred to as being "in the zone." The skill becomes effortless, and to the outside observer, it looks as if they were born to do this and they are of a special breed. Yet on further investigation, you will find out that their skill is the result of repeated practice. Malcolm Gladwell, in *Outliers: The Story of Success*, describes the ten-thousand-hour rule, which is the theory that to reach the level of expert in any skill, it takes at minimum ten thousand hours of focused practice.

The four stages of learning help us to see why it's so important to allow the time and effort to let change happen. Be open minded so that you can adapt and grow. Change is constant, so if you're not part of that change, you will become a victim of it instead. At first, change will not seem easy and it will be cumbersome, but, after dedicated and focused effort, you eventually will move into the final stages of effortless patterning and integration.

External Information

We receive about one billion bits of information each second through our senses. Just the input to the brain from the eyes alone equals ten thousand bits per second. Right now, as you read this, until I mention it, you are unaware of the temperature of the room; the noise of nearby appliances or equipment; the clothing on your back; the sock around your ankle; the waistband of your underwear; the earrings in your ear; the ring on your finger. These have all been diminished to allow you to focus on what's most important. Unless these various items become a problem for us or pose some danger, we remain oblivious to their presence and zero in on what seems to be most significant at the moment.

This brings me to the main point: How do we process all this incoming information in order to have it make sense and allow us to move through our surroundings? Human beings have a unique way of processing and defining the meaning of the world around us. The human brain is an amazingly engineered machine, and if it's used wisely and efficiently, we can achieve incredible things. However, like any finely tuned machine, in order to get the best out of it, you must have the proper information manual for its function. Through my study of neurolinguistic programming, human psychology, and the latest research on the function of the brain, I have gathered up a number of effective strategies in order to effectively operate this thing between our ears.

Generalizations, Deletions, and Distortions

Since we've established that human beings receive a billion bits of information each and every second of the day, let's look at what happens to that information once it's received by the brain. Human beings have an astonishing ability to narrow down the complex into the simple. In order to integrate and assimilate all the information, we need to sort it and decipher what's important and what's not. According to Richard Bandler and John Grinder, the creators of neurolinguistic programming (NLP), in order to break down the flood of incoming input into usable and contextual information, we humans inherently do three things: we generalize, delete, and distort incoming information. Just by listening to someone speak, you can begin to follow the automatic sorting of information using these three methods in order to keep it simple and understandable inside our heads.

Generalizations

When we generalize, we tend to use words that are all-encompassing. "Every time," "everywhere," and "always" are just a few of the terms we use when we generalize. Those who tend to generalize often struggle with feeling stressed and overwhelmed, which is usually because they are hearing their own defeating self-talk. Not only do we express our feelings to the world around us, but, most importantly, we also hear feedback via our own internal self-talk. Take the mother who gets overwhelmed by thinking and voicing that she is responsible for everything and that everything depends on her if it is to get done. She soon finds herself overwhelmed by her daily to-do list. In this case, the solution is to have her move from generalization to percent specification. Have her see her reality for what it is and define exactly what needs to be done to get the outcome she really wants. For example, what she really wants is to have a happy and balanced home for her family. Getting frustrated and angry because she didn't get "everything" done makes her impatient and temperamental with her family—causing her to move much farther away from the outcome she really wanted, leading to even more feelings of guilt and shame.

Let's take a common phrase that is the epitome of generalized language. Have you ever heard or repeated the words "Bad things always happen in threes"? It will likely prove itself true because we begin to search for all evidences of "bad things always happening" in order to fulfill this prophecy. We find ourselves using other people's misfortunes to add to our list and even end up transforming good events into bad in order to support our beliefs. The fact is that things don't happen in any predetermined number; things just happen. It's all how you look at it.

I once had a client tell me that anyone who was late, even just a few minutes, led her to assume that person was untrustworthy. What kind of past beliefs and generalizations did she set up in her head involving time and trust? Did this mean that when she was late, she was untrustworthy, too? Can you imagine living in her world where everything had to be aligned in order to allow her to reach her destination on time? Traffic, appointments, delays—all must have been a major source of stress. Never mind the pressure she must have placed on those around her who would be constantly under the microscope of trying to keep her trust and, therefore, her love. The conditions we set up in our heads have a profound effect not only on ourselves but on those close to us as well.

Deletions

When we delete information, we tend to only have a small segment of the true representation of the real experience. The only issue in this situation is that we must be mindful of deleting important information that we can use to create a much more empowering and supportive reality. I once heard a recount of a party that was attended by two of my coaching clients. They happened to be friends and were both present at the same party. The first client recounted that the party was not so great. The entertainment and food were lacking, and she felt as if the service was slow. My other client had another version of the same party. She said the entertainment was amazing, the food was plentiful, and the service was excellent. Why would two people have such different realities? Well, after speaking with the second client, I found out that my first client was late getting to the party, which left her with very little food, no entertainment, and waiters who were busy cleaning up so they didn't have time to pay attention to her. If I were to get only one view of the party, I would have a different picture of what really went on that night. In this example, in order to have the story be congruent with her beliefs about the event, my first client deleted the entire story of the late arrival, therefore painting a wholly different picture in her reality. When my client recounted the story, it was expressed with complete conviction and belief, letting me know that this was now her truth as she knew it. This example should have you wondering what stories you've told yourself with conviction that may not be leading you to the empowerment you need to achieve your greatness.

We delete information on a daily basis, which is why I suggest that you question your beliefs surrounding any roadblocks you may have created to block you from having everything you desire in life. Did your teacher in junior high really have it out for you, or did you delete the part about your consistent habit of not having your assignments done on time? What if you gave more of your time and energy to studying for that test instead of hanging out with your friends or constantly being distracted by social media or the TV? Could you have passed that exam if you either studied harder or went in for extra help, or do you think it's really true that you're not as smart as the other people in the class who are passing with flying colors? Does the boss really have it out for you, or is it that you've missed the deadline on a few assignments and are often late running into the office each morning, so now you have compromised the trust and confidence that people above you needed to have in order to give you the bigger and more important jobs?

In order to reach a balanced state with our mental essence, we must develop the habit of being real with ourselves and questioning many of our long-standing beliefs. The primary reason why this is a good exercise is that once we've deleted and embellished a story in our heads, it becomes our set blueprint for the world around us, eventually guiding and affecting our entire life's decisions and direction. As the Biblical saying goes, "[T]he truth will set you free."

Distortions

Distortion of our experience can also be helpful in processing information, but we sometimes distort our experience of reality to one that doesn't serve our greatness. Distortion occurs when people twist their perception of an experience in order to have it match up with the reality or blueprint they have installed in their heads. In the case of individuals using distortion, you will find that they tend to make hasty assumptions and draw unwarranted conclusions about an experience. Depending on their cultural backgrounds, past experiences, and belief systems, they will tend to distort their reality, creating stress, tension, and a daunting view of the world and their situations.

People who distort their reality are those who are constantly looking for reasons to be upset in any given situation. They can find trouble in paradise. This usually stems from a sense of constantly striving and never measuring up, so they are afraid to be vulnerable enough to allow themselves to be happy. They spend their time distorting various experiences, such as the way someone looks at them, a certain comment that was made in a general sense but interpreted as directed at them, or a joke that was made to an entire group but causes them to take personal offense. These people have a certain blueprint of how the world should be, and they will distort any scenario to have it match up to their beliefs.

These three—generalizations, deletions, and distortions—are the most frequently used filters in our daily interactions as we attempt to manipulate the world around us. If we are to achieve true balance in our mental essences, then we need to be aware of the use of these three filters so we can create a more empowering reality for ourselves and those around us. The stress we feel is subjective, and it is 100 percent dictated by how we process information. Proper use of our language, both outer and inner language, can be the key to finding peace and balance in our lives.

Subliminal Influences on Your Reality

Slick advertisers are completely aware of the power of subliminal messages. We are constantly bombarded by incoming under-the-radar messages that cause us to make unconscious decisions. We rarely ever buy items we need; we buy on the basis of wants and immediate gratification. For example, would you admit that getting safely from point A to point B should be our number-one goal when purchasing a vehicle? Yet, we all know that we are driven by a subliminal affinity for the bells, whistles, and brand names of the most popular and usually the most expensive cars in order to fulfill our unconscious desires, which are primarily driven by the embedded messages in much of our advertising over many years and decades. In *Subliminal: How Your Unconscious Mind Rules Your Behavior*,

Leonard Mlodinow writes that the subliminal messages coming into our nervous systems are immense and constant. We are only aware of 5 percent of all incoming information, while the other 95 percent is below our awareness and yet has a huge influence on our psychology. A third of the brain is dedicated to visual processing; this is important because the subliminal information coming into our consciousness is primarily passing through our visual system.

Here is what I want you to take away: we must be mindful to guard the doorway to our minds by actively scrutinizing what we decide to focus on and what we choose to entertain us through our senses, especially by way of our visual input. It's no wonder many of our seniors have such a negative worldview—many seniors regularly watch the news at least three times per day, and more importantly, at night when they are most relaxed and open to both visual and auditory stimuli. Here is my strong suggestion to you: take inventory of your own habitual practices to ensure that you are guarding the entrance to your mind. Once your habitual practices become unconscious programming, it takes a great deal of energy and effort to correct your course to one that serves you and doesn't defeat you, moving you even further away from your greatness.

Inner Workings of the Mind

We could never effectively achieve balance in the mental essence without thinking about the inner workings of the mind itself. The mind can be separated into two categories, the conscious and subconscious. When we attempt to figure out what's going on within the mind, we must include both divisions. We must also consider an important structure within the brain called the *prefrontal cortex*, which has a profound effect on what gets fed into the conscious and subconscious. The prefrontal cortex is part of our brain's cortex, or the outer layer of brain tissue, and it is responsible for all of our executive functions. The prefrontal cortex helps us to function effectively in the world around us. You will hear much more on this important structure later because it has a profound effect on our emotional balance due to its link to the emotional centers of our brains. I also mention this structure because there are certain specific mental conditioning exercises that can have a profound effect on its overall structure and function.

As astonishing and powerful as our brains are, we, unfortunately, did not get the owner's manual to this complex and amazing machinery between our ears. Science, philosophy, and Buddhist practice have begun to investigate the power we have to make significant changes within the brain structure and function, and we are just scratching the surface when it comes to figuring out the capabilities of our minds and how we can affect them both negatively and positively. Mastering our mental essences is all about being mindful of how we can shape and guide the brain and, therefore, the mind in order to effectively help us to achieve our greatest selves.

The Conscious Mind

The conscious and subconscious minds have been the focus of psychologists and philosophers for centuries. Sigmund Freud, in his *Theory of Personality*, gives the most famous definition of the conscious mind. He states that the conscious mind can be defined as everything inside our awareness. This definition can include the sensations we feel, the perceptions, and the conscious thoughts we fantasize about on a daily basis. Associated with the conscious mind is also the preconscious, which processes anything we are not presently thinking about but can easily be brought to our awareness.

The conscious mind can be considered the tool for creating the world around us. This is the part of our brains that gives us the ability to choose the quality of the thoughts we produce at each and every second of our lives. The key here is to realize that you have a choice of what gets in and what you allow to dominate your conscious thinking. At every moment of our day, we are exercising choices as to what thoughts would best serve our needs for that given scenario.

In his book *Essentials of Managing Stress*, Brian Luke Seaward documents that the conscious mind operates at about 10 to 12 percent of the mind's total capacity. On the Internet, you may have seen the frequently published image of an iceberg with the relatively small tip showing above the water and the massive chunk that lies below. This is a great metaphor to represent the conscious mind, which relates to the tip of the iceberg, only taking up 10 to 12 percent of the mass, while the subconscious mind, which is depicted as the massive ice chunk underwater, takes up the remaining 88 to 90 percent.

Under normal circumstances, the conscious mind is mainly active in our waking life, busily receiving and sorting the fifty to sixty thousand thoughts and billions of bits of incoming stimuli from the outside environment and our bodily sensations. During sleep, the activity decreases in order for us to assimilate, integrate, and process our day's experiences. The conscious mind has no capacity for holding memory and is only responsible for keeping us in the present moment.

Understanding the conscious mind is no easy feat, but, for our purposes, we will keep it simple by focusing on just one primary area of the brain called the prefrontal cortex. The prefrontal cortex is responsible for our executive functioning, meaning that it is the master conductor to the rest of the brain's function. We consciously live through the prefrontal cortex; it's involved in decision making, goal setting, altruism, helping us in social situations by choosing appropriate actions, producing deep thoughts, and expressing our creativity. I think you would agree that the optimal functioning of the prefrontal cortex just about covers everything we need to live out our greatness.

The Subconscious Mind

The subconscious mind, responsible for dictating anywhere from 88 to 90 percent of our reality, uses a large percentage of the energy allotted to the brain. The storage capacity of the subconscious mind has not yet been quantified, but the limits of its ability to store memories seem infinite. Some alternative medicine practitioners, spiritual healers, and hypnotists say that in the subconscious mind can be found not only memories from childhood but also memories from past lives. Most interesting is that the subconscious mind is timeless in that it does not adhere to the concept of time, which explains why we often struggle with ridding ourselves of childhood memories and we can easily revert back to childlike behaviors if triggered by any event resembling an old and significant experience we faced in childhood, even though the event was sitting quietly below our conscious awareness for years or even decades.

The subconscious mind plays a key role in creating the map we have to guide us through our world. It does this by working hard to fill in the gaps in our consciousness and our experience of the world around us, and since we process the world through our five senses, which are not always the most reliable sources, we tend to get only a small portion of the entire experience. For example, within the construction of the human visual system, we have an inherent weakness: we possess a natural blind spot as our eyes track the environment and read information. It is not a smooth and seamless flow—we have jumps from one fixation point to the other called *saccades*. This means that at any time during our visual processing of our environment, we are missing information about our experience. Nature has tried its best to mitigate this weakness through certain supporting systems, but it still leaves us with room for errors. Part of that support system is that the unconscious processing will often automatically fill in these gaps of information by going into our past experiences, giving us the ability to get the gist of the situation and make an appropriate decision on how we should respond. The same is true for the auditory system in that we only have to hear a partial version of any information and the subconscious dives in to fill in the blanks. This is important to us as we continuously count on our senses to guide us away from danger and toward survival.

The subconscious mind is associated with the areas of the brain containing emotions and memories. These two areas, the *amygdala* (responsible for our emotions) and the *hippocampus* (the storehouse for all our memories), are anatomically and functionally linked. It's no wonder certain memories can lead to an instantaneous trigger to an emotional reaction and certain emotional experiences can also trigger stored memories from long ago. Also associated with these two subconscious brain centers is the area for smell. The olfactory nerves have a direct route to the brain and can also trigger past memories and strong emotion. Have you ever noticed how certain smells can instantly trigger past memories? Both negative and positive memories can be aroused just through the sense of smell.

The subconscious mind never sleeps and is constantly involved in processing and storing incoming information. Good memories, bad memories, and even painful memories that may harm us are sorted and stored until needed at a later date, or sometimes never to be consciously accessed again. There are many times in my practice that I deal with people who have suffered traumatic events in their lives, but the need to move on and effectively get through their lives on a daily basis and in a healthy and productive manner has caused them to store those memories away. Sometimes the place of storage may be in the body's tissues, making it that much harder to find relief of their pain due to a subconscious link to the traumatic past experience. For some of my clients, that recurring and nagging shoulder or back pain can have a strong correlation to some situation that involves confronting a past negative experience

Since most of our automatic survival mechanisms, such as the control centers for fight, flight, food, and sex, are controlled within the areas associated with the subconscious mind, stimulation and activation of the subconscious can have a profound and deleterious effect on the body as a whole. This is why it's so important to take inventory, clean up, and become aware of our subconscious processing so we can achieve balance of the mental essence. Our ultimate goal is that we gain control of our persistent and consistent thoughts within our conscious mind. Thoughts lead to feelings, and prolonged feelings lead eventually to a physiological, full-body reaction.

Your Greatness Exercise:
How to Balance Your Mental Essence

All that information is well and good, but how do we use it in a practical manner? How do we take this knowledge of the brain and its intricate processes and use it to our advantage?

Meditation

There's really nothing more powerful for laying down the tracks for effective control of the mind than *meditation*. Numerous studies have now shown the effect of meditation in actually changing the structure of the brain and, therefore, its overall function. Frequent meditation sessions allow you to become detached from your problems and worries, permitting you to view them from a more manageable perspective. Regular meditation calms the mind and releases tension from the body, thereby facilitating a better sense of clarity and focus in order to gain control and a deeper sense of self.

How do you meditate? Meditation may sound easy, but, for many, it's a chore trying to quiet the mind. As soon as there's some sense of quiet, it's like a green light for the mind to start running like a squirrel trying to cross a busy road; back and forth, back and forth it goes, undecided and frantic, as the squirrel (your mind) attempts to make a decision on which way to go. This can be a frustrating and futile process, often leading to defeat. Those people who are new to meditation frequently find that either they become more frustrated than they were before or they simply get distracted, and some eventually fall asleep.

So what are the steps to easily implementing a regular meditation practice? The first thing to do is to designate a time and sacred space for meditation that you know you can always retreat to when needed. Now, we can move on to the actual practical steps to meditation:

> Step one: Simply sit in a comfortable posture. Not too comfortable, such as being reclined or lying down and supported by pillows and cushions. This typically lends to falling asleep and losing focus on your meditation practice. But

you do want to be comfortable enough to maintain at least ten to thirty minutes or more of sustained, quiet sitting.

Step two: The goal is simple; your primary focus will be on your breath. The procedure is that you follow your breath as it enters your nose and travels through your throat, filling your chest with air until it forces the breath to be transferred down to your abdomen. This can be felt as an expansion of the abdomen as it begins to fill. As you continue to follow the breath as it descends, you will feel it travel even farther down toward your pelvic floor. This can also be felt as a light but definite downward pressure on the floor of your pelvis. When you're finally able to connect with this breath, you will become aware of the sensation of your breath deep to your lower extremities.

Once you are able to successfully and easily visualize this process occurring deep inside you, then you're there! You've discovered the elusive secret to meditation. The magic of this meditative process is that when you breathe, you have to realize you're in touch with the most powerful thing within your possession, the breath. Breath signifies life at its essence. When we are born, we take our first breath, and when we die, we exhale our last. In between, it's all about the efficient usage of our breath. Additionally, the breath also indicates your ability to be present within the moment. If you are aware of your breath, then that means you are present within your body right where you are. You're neither in the past nor in the future, just present and witnessing all the magic, and that's powerful!

Journaling

The second secret to gaining control of the mental essence is *journaling*. Journaling helps you to get a bird's-eye view of your problem or roadblock. Have you ever noticed how easy it is to give someone advice, but you constantly struggle to find a way out of your own dilemma? This is because when you're in the problem, you develop what can be referred to as *myopic vision*. You zero in on the problem and not the solution, even if the solution is right under your nose. Journaling your feelings enables you to step back and take a look at your situation from a much more empowering vantage point. At this vantage point, you can often find solutions where it previously looked like none existed. Journaling is a key tool in cognitive behavioral therapy. Patients are given the task of journaling their feelings about any given situation the moment it arises. That way, they can become detached from their circumstances in order to be less emotional and connected.

So how do you journal, and what should you write about? Just about anything you feel. You can write in short forms, include pictures, drawings, charts, cartoons, jargon, trendy words, etc. There really are no regulations on how to write in YOUR journal. This is your time to release all inhibitions and avoid all rules about what and how to write. Your journal is a great way to just express everything you're feeling and struggling with inside your head. No one has to see it; you never have to share it with someone. It's your place to dump it all out. Have fun!

Affirmations

The third most powerful secret to gaining a powerful mental essence is *affirmations*! Mahatma Gandhi said, "Your beliefs become your thoughts, your thoughts become your words, your words become your actions." What we say to ourselves on a consistent basis helps in a tremendous way to form our character and our belief systems. The biggest believer and proponent of this theory was Muhammad Ali, who was known for repeating the words "I am the greatest!" Many thought this was coming from a place of ego, but Muhammad understood that if he wanted to do the impossible, he had to continually engrain a strong belief that he was the greatest; now many would argue that he was the major game changer of his time and a legend in the game of boxing and beyond.

Whether we know it or not, we are constantly creating our worlds through the language we use both verbally and inside our heads. Most of the time, the reality we are creating is based on a negative viewpoint. We can often catch ourselves berating our choices and decisions. We are our worst critics. We don't even have to worry about outside influences; the real enemy is often within.

When you actively choose to install positive affirmations, they have the effect of changing your life, and these changes you will achieve will be from the core, the place where true long-lasting changes occur. You can think of affirmations as if your words were a continuous stream of clear water being poured into a jug of colored water, where as time goes by and the water remains consistently poured in, the colored water begins to be diluted, eventually becoming consumed by the continuous infusion of the clear water. With continuous infusion of your daily positive affirmations, your negative thought patterns will begin to be diluted by ones that are more capable of having you finally achieve your greatest self.

Language Patterns

Just like the effect that affirmations have on our ability to change our affinity for the negative, watching our *language patterns* is key to supporting the permanent changes we've installed through our affirmations. One of the first steps in my coaching process with my clients is to monitor their language patterns. Words such as "try," "should," and "have to" are just some of the words that play a subtle role in sabotaging the changes we want to make.

When you are looking to make some serious changes in your life, the word "try" is an indication that you are not 100 percent committed to your goal. "Try" gives you an out, just in case the road gets a little tough or you're being challenged. The words "should" and "have to" are stress words, and they suggest to the subconscious mind that you have no choice in the matter; who doesn't love to have choices? I have to lose weight—versus I want to lose weight—has a whole different meaning to the subconscious mind. Words that signify a lack of choice in any given situation will easily lead to resistance and eventual failure. Do you remember when you were told that you should eat your veggies or you should clean your room?

Your language patterns are created throughout your entire life history. Some of them were conscious, and some were unconscious; it all depended on your environment, social life, past life experiences, beliefs, and values. The effect of the above influences is often insidious but equally profound in creating your reality and determining how far you will eventually go in life. I am coaching you to become conscious of the words you use throughout your daily interactions with others and especially your interaction with yourself. You will, at first, find it extremely difficult to catch yourself using these words. You will be amazed at how many times you actually do participate in self-defeating programming; if you are mindful of the effects your words have on you, you will begin to see how vital it is to monitor and correct your language patterns.

Using the information above, we can start to develop an effective plan of action in order to regain balance in our mental essence and, therefore, balance in our lives in general. The brain is plastic, which simply means that the brain's main function is to learn and adapt to changes. When equipped with this knowledge, the primary motivation for implementing these strategies in your daily routine and in your life is that you can rest assured that with constant input of the right information, you can change your entire world one hundred and eighty degrees in what will seem like an instant! It really doesn't matter where you started and how many mistakes or failures you've had over your lifetime; what matters is what you do with your present moment. Each time we are able to make decisions that lead us to where we eventually want to end up, we are shaping and rearranging our entire future. This, you can be assured, is true.

5

Emotional Essence

A few years ago, a client walked into my clinic. He was an elite athlete approaching the top of his game but was feeling frustrated that he couldn't figure out his inability to break through to finally reach what he felt was his greatness. Every so often, he would flirt with greatness, but he was pulled back into mediocrity every time. He had all the genetics, skills, and abilities to reach that next level, and he knew that other competitors ahead of him were less talented and less naturally gifted for achieving greatness, but it didn't matter. He watched for years as many bypassed him to take what he believed was his place in the top echelon of this sport.

Each time he attempted to make a run for the top spot, he somehow became hurt, or some other "bad luck" circumstance would stop his drive to reach the end goal. He had now assumed the mentality that it is what it is and this must be his lot in life. Basically, he had developed the condition of *learned helplessness*, which I discussed in chapter 1. Aptly named by American psychologist Martin E. P. Seligman, the term describes the mental state that individuals develop who have repeatedly gone through what they perceive to be adverse situations and have become unable or unwilling to persevere in order to get to their goal. This is usually because they now believe that their situation is beyond their ability to rise above and the problems seem insurmountable. They begin to develop an impoverished mindset that leaves them feeling helpless and disempowered to change their circumstances.

With this kind of mental programming running constantly in the background, it would be impossible for my client to find and claim his true greatness. After some questioning and delving deeper into his history, he revealed to me that he had a violent and turbulent upbringing with an alcoholic father who was constantly out of work. My client was from the roughest part of his hometown, and he experienced poverty his entire childhood. He was also ridiculed in school and made to feel as if he was incapable of performing on an academic level. He avoided making friends in order to avoid bringing someone home to meet his family. As he kept his home life a secret, these circumstances became his whole reality and formed the background to his life's story. He carried the heavy weight of shame his entire life. The emotion of shame was such a profound part of his psyche that whatever happened to him, good or bad, contributed to his deep-seated inability to feel good about himself or feel as if he deserved to touch his own personal greatness.

The shame he felt about the events in his past played a massive part in keeping him in mediocrity and fear. He feared that if he became vulnerable enough to expose himself by expressing his true personal greatness, someone would eventually find out about his innate weaknesses—which were magnified in his mind due to his belief about his past. He had associated going from good to great with being even more vulnerable to the critique and invasion of his private life. This underlying fear wreaked havoc in his life by constantly rearing its ugly head during times when he was faced with moving beyond mediocrity.

I am certain that his story is a common one in our society. Many of us walk around with our own "dirty little secrets" or hidden shame that keeps us from going toward our greatness full-on 100 percent. Your version of the dirty little secret doesn't have to read like my client's did; what I've found is that, no matter the degree of the event, it's all relative in the subconscious mind and a secret shame is the same for everyone. It could be based on real events, or it could easily have been created by a perception that was further supported by a few circumstances that confirmed your distorted view. Either way, it's yours to live with, and if it's not identified and eradicated, then it becomes a cancer to your soul, as it metastasizes to other areas of your life and retards your ability to achieve peak performance. When do you know you have contracted this deep-seated virus? When you're faced with that moment when the pressure to achieve is at its summit, or when you're standing in front of a golden opportunity, and you find that you're frozen, unable to take the first step into the light of your greatness.

In this chapter, the goal is to inform you that we've been equipped with the capacity to change our habitually negative and erratic emotional reactions. With time and mindful, deliberate practice, we don't have to be held hostage by our emotions; we can be in control. Negative emotions have long been associated with irrationality and unpredictability. They often spring out of us without a moment's notice and with the slightest provocation. These emotional outbursts can lead to a number of deleterious mental and physical reactions that seem to be out of our control, but, when you are armed with the information you will receive from this chapter, you will move from being a victim to a victor over your circumstances.

Anatomy of the Emotional Essence:

How We Store and Process Our External World

Since we could dig endlessly into the copious amounts of research on the brain and nervous system, which are key to the storage and processing of our emotions, I am going to limit the information to a few key areas of the brain that I've found to be essential to achieving emotional wellness and stability. These are also the areas of the brain where, with consistent focus and practice, we can make profound and positive changes: the prefrontal cortex, the amygdala, and the hippocampus. To gain control of any emotional state, we must achieve balance and change the patterns we feed into these three regions. I will also focus on two emotional states—shame and guilt—that are frequently the underlying cause of our tendency to stay in mediocrity. Finally, we will look at a very important concept referred to as *schema*. Collectively, these factors are often the root problem keeping us from expressing our greatness.

We all experience negative emotions in our lives; there's no getting away from them. Besides, we often need our emotions in order to get important things done or to drive us up and over the numerous obstacles we meet on the way to our destinations. The real goal is to realize that you have a choice of how and when to react in any given situation so you can achieve your desired results. Aristotle, in his *Nichomachean Ethics*, wrote: "Anyone can become angry—that is easy. But to be angry with the right person, to the right degree, at the right time, for the right purpose, and in the right way—that is not easy."

Brain Regions Involved in Emotional States:

Prefrontal Cortex

Let's start with the prefrontal cortex. As the name states, this area of the brain is located in the front and uppermost part of the brain and is associated with higher consciousness, decision making, setting and achieving goals, cognition, and a whole host of higher-level functioning. Although emotions have always been primarily associated with the amygdala, the prefrontal cortex also has strong links to the emotional centers of the brain. The prefrontal cortex and the limbic system send information between each other to maintain a functional and healthy emotional state. In particular, the left prefrontal cortex has been shown to be responsible for inhibition of signals travelling to the amygdala during emotional reactions. Optimal functioning of the left prefrontal cortex is essential to building resiliency during prolonged emotional states and ensuring recovery from strong periods of emotional input.

According to Richard Davidson and Sharon Begley in *The Emotional Life of Your Brain*:

> Those people who are fast to recover from adversity and are thus extremely resilient show strong activation of the left prefrontal cortex in response to setbacks and have strong connections of the left prefrontal cortex and the amygdala. By dampening down the amygdala, the prefrontal cortex is able to quiet the signals associated with negative emotions, enabling the brain to plan and act effectively without being distracted by negative emotions.

Now, how many of us wouldn't wish we could just set back the clock and rewind the entire event to a time before we reacted because of emotions? This is a key skill in any scenario; whether personal, business, sports, or relationships, being in control and strengthening our filter against overreaction is key to gaining balance in our emotional essences.

Limbic System

The limbic system is a complex and varied group of neural circuitry that has connections to numerous parts of the brain. The limbic system is the governor of most of our emotional lives and interactions. Within the group of nerves in the limbic system are the amygdala and hippocampus, which are intimately related and connected anatomically. These two areas are responsible for our emotions and memories, two very important aspects of our inability to let go of negative emotional events and the dark energy that is often associated with them. Their interrelation explains why certain memories stir up such strong emotions, even when you thought you were free of them.

Amygdala

The amygdala is located in the lower portion of the brain. Although only about the size and shape of an almond, this incredible structure packs a powerful punch. The amygdala is known for being the seat of our emotions and has associations with a number of other areas of the brain. The amygdala is part of the older and more rudimentary part of the brain, just above the brainstem. Due to its location on the spine, it is prone to immediate stimulation and activation from the external environment—a bottom-up transmission of signals. In other words, external stimulations—touching, being touched, pain, and so on—can easily stir an emotional reaction before our prefrontal cortex can have a say in the matter. It's no wonder that when people experience chronic pain for a prolonged period of time, it becomes more difficult for them to give adequate feedback to the degree of pain they feel. They are thought to be hyper-sensitized to pain. This kind of innate reaction can be to your benefit when you consider those times when you need to quickly react to external stimuli. This speedy response has been essential to our survival through millions of years of evolution.

"Amygdala Hijacking"

Have you ever had one of those times when you were completely out of control? So much that no matter what you did, you could see yourself doing the act but felt that you were completely unable to stop? We've all heard of those people who escape conviction for a serious crime by claiming they were in distress and emotional at the time; they claim to be acting from a place outside of themselves and beyond their ability to control it.

Take a client of mine, Simone M., who experienced a major and debilitating accident at the hands of a careless driver some three years prior to seeing me. While she carefully rode her bicycle down a side street in her town, mindful of passing traffic, a young driver clipped her tire and sent her over her handlebars. She landed on her head and shoulder, and she suffered for quite some time with headaches and shoulder pain. When she came to me, she was finally seeing some improvement in her condition, but, due to the resentment she felt over the accident, there was a great deal of underlying emotional trauma as well. She managed to maintain herself at a healthy and functional level, but when you started to dig deeper into conversations about the accident, then the emotional scars became visible.

One day, as she was crossing through a shopping center parking lot, she was startled when a driver abruptly reversed his car without checking his blind spots as she passed close by. As would be expected, she was frightened by the close call. This minor incident, which in typical circumstances would be forgiven and chalked up to a common mishap, sent her into a rage as she was taken back to the incident three years prior. Her hippocampus, the area of past memories, triggered her amygdala to stir up an emotional reaction that would be enough to stimulate the fight-or-flight response. In this case, the memory and stored-up trauma caused her to fly into fight mode, whereby the amygdala hijacked the prefrontal cortex and took it hostage.

She was enraged and found that she was driven to hysterically banging on the driver's car. She later said she could see herself freaking out excessively but could not help herself to stop. The driver was clearly stunned at the reaction and did not leave the car. After what seemed to her like a period of minutes but was actually only a few seconds, she managed to get hold of herself and began to calm down. Luckily, there were only minor damages to his car in the form of small indentations from her fists, and because it was his work vehicle and had a few previous dents, he did not get out to confront her. Instead, he remained in his car, possibly also traumatized from this apparently crazy person. As she saw him pick up his cellular phone, she immediately left the scene of the incident.

This is the power of an emotional hijacking by the limbic system. Deep underlying memories and emotions that have not been effectively dealt with can lie dormant until some kind of provocation. The trigger that releases the stored memories can be minor or major in nature, but, to the person experiencing the emotion, caught in the moment, the reaction will seem justified and even rationalized as appropriate. The person may be blinded by rage or the need to take flight or shut down to avoid dealing with the situation.

Hippocampus

When I first arrived in Canada from Jamaica, I was amazed at all the sights and sounds, the smell of the crisp and fresh Canadian air, and the look of the huge, white flakes of fluffy snow as they wafted down to cover the ground. Everything was new and wondrous, and there was so much to get used to. The experience still lingers in my mind and conjures up such great emotions. I want to touch on an incident that had a profound effect on me and provides a deeper understanding of the power of memory and its emotional connection.

I was about ten years old, and I had only been in Canada for about a year. It was the end of June, and, like most schools in North America, we were involved in the usual intramural sporting competitions with students competing in various sporting events throughout the day. There was also a barbeque with free hotdogs and hamburgers. I was dying to try a hot dog, which I prepared with care as I spread on my condiments. Now, as funny as this may sound, I started to apply to my bun what I thought was butter, yes, butter on my hot dog bun; don't judge me. It turned out to be mustard! I can look back now and say of course mustard, what else? But, back then, it was all new to me, and there is nothing like anticipating one thing and getting something else. This was quite a rude awakening to my taste buds.

I felt nauseous and on the verge of vomiting as my stomach and senses went into rebellion. It would take thirty years before I stopped being negatively aroused by the sight and smell of mustard.

One negative exposure to a perfectly tasteful spice shaped my reality in such a way that it caused me three decades of inappropriate responses. This is the power of the hippocampus and our limbic system on display. Although this response is primarily a protective mechanism and very useful, inappropriate and repeated exposure to a negative stimulus can wreak havoc on our lives.

The hippocampus is an area of the brain with an intimate relationship with the amygdala, as the hippocampus's horseshoe-shaped formation sits atop the amygdala, hugging and draping the almond-shaped structure on both sides of the brain. The hippocampus is involved in the formation, organization, and storage of memories. Due to its connection with the amygdala and its function as part of the limbic system, the hippocampus has a strong association with creating and sorting our emotions. Incoming information caused by sights, sounds, and smells also has an impact on the overall function of the hippocampus.

Why is this so significant? With this information in mind, you know how important it is to be mindful and sensitive of your environment when creating your reality. To expand even further, it's no wonder some habits are so hard to quit—most times we change only one variable of our habits, forgetting about the effect that the environment and all its sensory information has on creating memories of the habit. In order to form any habit, it takes a repetition of the action. This repetition is a form of learning, imprinting, and memorization, which involves activation of the hippocampus.

Guilt and Shame

My clients were in their mid-fifties, an average, working, middle-class couple raising two teenaged boys. She was a bank teller, and he was an engineer for a local planning and design company.

Due to his executive position, he worked fairly long hours, and his wife did an average forty-hour work week. They both juggled to attain the elusive life balance. Despite his crazy hours at work, he tried as much as he could to be engaged in his kids' lives. When he could, he coached his sons' hockey and soccer teams and tried his best to make every event, as did his wife. Their story was no different than the average couple's as they tried to raise two successful future adults who would eventually lead fulfilling lives with their own families and friends.

Everything appeared to be on track. The boys, two years apart, seemed to be average teenagers with average teenage issues. Then, one evening, while they were enjoying a quiet moment at home, my clients heard an unexpected knock at the door. They were met with a sight no parent wants to see—the police—and the officers had that business-like look on their faces. This wasn't a courtesy call. It was to inform my clients that there had been an armed robbery and their oldest son had been arrested as the main suspect.

They went through the usual shock and disbelief that they were now the parents of a felon. They racked their brains as to how their child, with all the comforts of a good life, could have done such a thing. They were devastated, and the reality of the event was compounded when they had to visit their child behind the barrier of the jail.

The event was such a traumatic time for my clients that it put a huge stress and tension on their lives and relationship as they struggled to understand how they could have missed the signs and signals. The guilt was tremendous, so much so that they constantly fought depression as they dealt with self-defeating thoughts and strong feelings of shame. What would their friends and associates say? Would everyone judge them as being failures as parents? Were they the worst parents in the world?

Despite raising both boys exactly the same, they could not help thinking they missed the boat on one of them, even though their other son—raised with the exact same principles, rules, guidelines, and opportunities—went on to be a successful and contributing member of society. As parents, though, we are always just about as happy as our saddest child. So, as would be expected, this couple couldn't help but think "What if?" as they struggled with guilt and shame. What if they had stopped and listened more? Paid more attention to him? Spent more time catering to his needs? They beat themselves up trying to find the missing link that caused him to go off track. It took them quite a few years before they came to grips with the fact that he made his own choices and his decision was based on satisfying his personal needs at that time. They did the best they could with what they had, and no one was to blame.

We all struggle with these two negative emotions, guilt and shame, in one way or another. It could be shame from spending patterns that place you in a continual financial crisis that leaves you unable to afford the little things you want and need in life. This kind of shame leaves your soul feeling small and powerless with a constant feeling of self-doubt and uncertainty. Or it could be the guilt you feel as a parent when you believe that you have not lived up to the ideal of the mother or father you think you could be, or that your culture thinks is the perfect model of a successful parent. We all go through the myriad of guilt and shame emotions throughout our lives. These kinds of feelings all lead us to view ourselves as less than our best and leave us in a state of mediocrity, self-doubt, and tension.

Here's a great way to summarize the emotions of guilt and shame and to know when we are experiencing either of the two, presented by Brene Brown in her book *The Gifts of Imperfection: Let Go of Who You Think You're Supposed to Be and Embrace Who You*

Are. She states that the majority of researchers who focus on guilt and shame agree that the difference between them is best defined in this way: when someone is experiencing guilt, the self-talk is typically "I did something bad," while those who experience shame struggle with the self-talk that states, "I am bad." One emotion is all about our behavior, while the other is all about who we are as a person.

It's quite easy to imagine how you might struggle with expressing your greatness if these two debilitating and quite frequent emotions continue to run in the background, creating your reality and stopping forward progress. These two emotions become like self-imposed anchors against your ability to fly to the levels where you are destined to go. Perhaps, like many of us, you feel guilt when your task list becomes unmanageable, then the shame of not being enough creeps in, and between the two, you're left feeling less than you could be. Your energy becomes stagnant as your mind, body, and soul start to feel as if you're moving through a thick sludge, and the cycle becomes a self-perpetuating monster.

Schema

"I lose, and I will always lose!" This was my first greeting from Ted, my thirty-eight-year-old, unemployed client. Ted had been unable to find a steady job and had found that he could only keep a job for three months at the most. Something always seemed to happen that disrupted his relationships at work. One time, it was that he didn't get along with a certain coworker, and, the next time, it was the environment at work. This had been going on since his adolescent years when "bad luck" got him in all kinds of trouble. The one thing I failed to hear when listening to his story was a sense of ownership for his life. Everything happened because of something outside of himself, and he was the victim in all cases. He just was not born under the right star, and everyone else seemed to have an easier path in life.

Ted was working exclusively from a *failure schema*. He had this underlying background story that painted his world gray and cloudy in every situation he encountered. He could never see the loving and undying support he received from those around him or the fact that he had the opportunity to change his paradigm and, therefore, his life with just one decision to turn it all around. The problem with his situation was that keeping the failure schema going also served a few of his needs for certainty, significance, love, and connection. By continually behaving this way, he had what he needed despite not being able to attain his autonomy and personal power.

Maladaptive Schemas

A schema is much like a blueprint that an architect creates for the general contractor to build from. With trust that the design is sound, the contractor begins to work, never thinking to question the information given to him or her. If there is an error in the blueprint, unless the contractor is versed in reading the architect's design, the error will go unnoticed. This flaw will only be revealed when the foundation is placed under repeated stress and tension or when one cataclysmic incident causes the entire structure to crumble.

A British psychologist named Fredric Bartlett put forth the *schema theory*. He suggested that a network of abstract mental structures creates our blueprint, or map of the world. There are four main concepts involved in Bartlett's schema therapy: early maladaptive theory, core emotional needs, schema mode, and maladaptive coping styles. Throughout our lives, we all experience these different styles of schemas in order to deal with the various scenarios we encounter.

In the maladaptive theory there are eighteen schemas, which are self-defeating models that we go to in any situation where we feel threatened. These self-defeating schemas are protective because they are developed in response to some kind of unmet need in childhood. Personally, having grown up in a tough environment in Kingston, Jamaica, I know that I've developed a number of schemas that at the time helped me to get through or get over my situation. However, I also realize that I had to take inventory of those schemas once my environment changed. The very same schemas that had helped me tremendously in the past are now maladaptive and are incongruent with my present reality and where I need to go with the rest of my journey. There have been so many times that I had to remind myself that a certain schema was not needed. I am safe now, and the walls can safely come down.

For our purposes, we will focus on just a few of these schemas that are often at the base of our inability to rise from mediocrity and into our personal greatness. We can know that these schemas are at work when we find that we habitually shrink back into security using a specific strategy as our safety net. Your schema can be confirmed as you find that you often overreact when you feel that you're faced with an uncertain situation. Your reactions in these cases frequently lead to results that further harm and hinder you rather than help you move toward personal growth. By knowing your specific schema, with focused intention and an effective strategy, you will be able to mitigate or even eliminate the effects of a schema gone wild. If you can raise your awareness with mindful and focused intention, you will be able to serve your core needs and emotions in order to finally reach a breakthrough.

Let's review a few of the often-visited schemas that may play a role in sabotaging your efforts to move toward your greatness:

- **Abandonment Schema**: In this schema, the person has a belief that he will not be supported when the chips are down. He has an unconscious feeling that he will be abandoned. This feeling can often spill over into his personal relationships as well.

- **Emotional Schema**: This person has a deep belief that those around her will not meet her emotional needs for nurturance, empathy, and protection.

- **Defective/Shame Schema**: This person has a feeling of being defective, a bad person, inferior, or unwanted. This self-defeating mentality causes the person to feel as if he is not capable of achieving his greatest self.

- **Social Isolation Schema**: This person has an underlying feeling that she is being excluded from most social situations. The feelings are often unwarranted and are at the forefront of her mind in many circumstances.

- **Failure Schema**: This person believes that he is destined to fail in anything he does, whether in sports, academics, or on a professional level.

- **Subjugation Schema**: This person is often known for giving up control to someone else. She often feels as if she is a slave being coerced into situations beyond her control. There are two types of subjugation—the subjugation of her own needs and the subjugation of her emotions. This person plays the victim in many scenarios and often bypasses the opportunity to step up to her greatness.

- **Hyper-criticalness Schema**: This person often calls himself a perfectionist, never able to achieve complete mastery of his craft due to an unrealistic, self-imposed level of success.

- **Approval-Seeking/Recognition Schema**: This person is constantly looking for approval and recognition from others around her. She is always seeking to be the center of attention and tries to fit into the crowd. She is often externally driven, gauging her self-esteem based on the opinions and feedback of others.

- **Negative/Pessimism Schema**: This person is always looking at the dark side of things. He constantly finds the negative in any situation, and that becomes the major focus of his attention.

The main issue with undiscovered or untreated schemas is that they end up being self-fulfilling prophecies, and they are ultimately counterproductive in getting out of mediocrity. However, schemas are treatable, and you can gain some control over them. This is not an easy process because your schemas run under your radar as they affect your decisions in crucial situations.

Your Greatness Exercise: Moving From Mediocrity to Greatness

How to Avoid Emotional Turmoil

Most of the causes of remaining in mediocrity can be linked to our inability as human beings to remain in the present moment. Very often, we find that our minds take a break away from the present to wander into their own little world. It's almost like we lose a sense of consciousness as the outside world slips away from us for a few minutes. It's not until we snap out of our daydream and mental movie-making that we realize we've lost a few moments of our lives to an imaginary dream world. There's nothing wrong with a healthy dose of mental imagery, but the issue is that when most of us go inside our heads to sort through our collections of mental experiences, we pick out the most emotionally disturbing and anxiety-ridden visualizations.

Here's the thing: in order to suffer anxiety, worry, doubt, fear, resentment, and regret, we must actively and by choice put our minds far ahead into the future, to some event that hasn't even happened yet, or to some time in the past that has been filled with an assortment of negative attachments that really occurred but have now been embellished to be even more monumental. Although the moment is long behind us, we are masters of reliving it in full-color Omnimax presentation. Not only that; we tend to go as far as adding the appropriate emotional content and physical manifestations, making the mental movie even more real and even more scary.

I want you to really get this because, once you do, you can harness all the power contained within your present space and time, as well as being able to achieve a sense of self-mastery and -control. Realize this—in the present moment, we are powerful and perfect. In the present moment, we are equal to everyone else we look up to or desire to emulate. In every second of each present moment that we can capture and preserve, we can use it to change our entire story to one built with optimism for our future. When we allow our minds to constantly shift into the past or the future, we tend to experience regret or anxiety, respectively.

I discovered this magic during my study and training in neurolinguistic programming—it's called *timeline therapy*. Within our nervous systems and unconscious minds, we humans have a unique way of storing and retrieving information. We tend to categorize and place our experiences in certain ways based on meaning and chronology. Where and how we store our experiences varies depending on the person, the event, and the circumstances surrounding the experience. In timeline therapy, through a series of questioning and evaluation, individuals reveal the location of an experience as they perceive it in their unconscious.

Ideally, your past should be behind you, your future in front of you, and you should be present in the here and now. This allows you to enjoy the moments in your life and not be off thinking about what went on in the past or what hasn't even happened yet in the future. Although this exercise involves a concept that seems intangible and esoteric to many people who try it for the first time, it's always interesting to me to see where people represent their idea of the location of their past, present, and future. Some people have their future timeline in their hearts, which means that, for them, just the thought of the future brings anxiety and an overwhelming emotional reaction. One person placed his past by his feet, which represented a reason to trip over his past each time he tried to move forward into the future. Another person placed her present moment within her chest, so that each time she tried to become present, she felt a sense of anxiety and pressure, which subconsciously caused her to avoid dealing with her present reality.

So as you can see, although this particular exercise involves theories that seem intangible, to each person, it's all about how you construct your reality in your unconscious mind, where you sort and store each experience. The way you organize your timeline can be the key to your ability to let your past be your teacher, move toward your greatness in the future, and become present in each moment so you can express yourself completely. The disorganization of your timeline can be the underlying roadblock to your forward progress and moving from living in mediocrity.

Below is a quick summary of the timeline and the associated emotions it conjures up. You can use the chart to match up some of the feelings you often spend time wrestling with and see if you catch yourself consistently hanging out in that zone. To take a quote from Jim Elliot, a Christian missionary: "Wherever you are, be all there!" That's our true goal in life and an effective way to release our brilliance.

Timeline Therapy

Past	Bitterness, resentment, guilt, shame, and blame.
Present	Freedom, peace, contentment, joy, and love.
Future	Stress, anxiety, worry, fear, and other overwhelming emotions.

I want you to ask yourself a simple question: Where do you organize your timeline? Take a minute to think about each category—past, future, and present. Ideally, when you think about past events in your life, where do you imagine them? Do you picture some event from the past in a specific position in your mind? Maybe you imagine it to the left or maybe even to the back or in front of you. Any way you imagine it, your past should be your teacher and not your jailer. Your future should pull you forward with excitement and enthusiasm, not fear and anxiety. In some NLP circles, the most ideal position for your recollection of the past is over the left shoulder, while other practitioners say the past can be to the left of you, almost like the fashion in which we read a book. As for your future, it would ideally be in front of you, just above your eyes, or in some cases to the right, depending on your method of storing and retrieving your experiences. These are the most suitable positions to imagine your future in order to prevent being blocked in your daily life and being unable to be present in each moment of creation. Finally, if you're asked to look within and become aware of the present moment, then you should easily be able to feel the breath of your body and a sense of clarity within your mind, as well as an awareness of your present being in a location just behind your forehead.

Working with Your Schemas

One of my clients stated to me that she could not control her emotions when it came to a certain group of people in her social life. Every time she got around them, she found that she reverted to feeling as if she was in elementary school and being excluded from the "in crowd." Even when she recounted the events of her experiences, she would become incensed at what she believed was unfair and unjust treatment by a particular person. The picture she painted was one of being alienated and left out of the plans of the group she was travelling with. The more she relived it, the more it sounded like something you would hear from a teenager, and the more she would revert to her years in grade school. Her anger and resentment were palpable. She had totally initiated her abandonment and social isolation schemas.

In order to effectively treat your schemas, you must catch yourself in the moment of a full-on schema attack. Learn to recognize the feelings that are brought on by your schema so you can catch them in their full effect. How do you know when your schema has gone out of hand and is in full-on attack mode? You can know that your maladaptive schema has been initiated when you find that your actions seem beyond your conscious control and your behavior brings you back to your irrational and volatile childlike self in an uncontrollable temper tantrum. When your schema is at work, you feel out of control, even though you are often fully aware of your actions and the possible outcomes. It becomes a battle between your rational and emotional minds as they jockey for front position in order to create a favorable and safe outcome. Observe your reaction, and aim to find the root of your maladaptive schema reaction. With continuous reflection and mindfulness regarding your feelings in the moment, you will become adept at linking your mood and behavior to one of the eighteen schemas. Once you can successfully do this, you will begin to shine the light on the hidden emotional monster.

Becoming the Observer

Have you ever noticed how you are able to effectively help everyone else but yourself when you're deep in your situation? When it comes to helping others, you have such clarity and unemotional attachment that you seem like an absolute genius in your response. Actually, you seem so brilliant that you begin to wonder when Oprah may call to get some of this genius. However, when it comes to your management of your own situation, it's akin to a train wreck, as you're completely consumed by your emotions, so much so that all you can see is the problem and no solution seems plausible.

Well, here is an effective solution: remove yourself from being the victim in your situation and become the victor of your situation instead. You do this by becoming the observer. By taking this stance, you are able to take an unemotional view of your problem. Distancing yourself allows you to adopt the same mentality as you would if you were helping a friend. You become unemotional and clear, allowing the answer to your problems to rise to your consciousness. By removing the emotional attachment, your rational and logical mind begins to be activated; this way, you can remove the negative labels that are often the key to keeping you hostage to your situation.

Body

6

Physical Essence

Let me introduce you to Brian, a hard-driving, thirty-four-year-old entrepreneur. He was an ex-athlete who, just a few years before, made working out and keeping fit a high priority. Recently, though, that passion slid to the background, replaced by a focus on growing his start-up advertising business. He felt that if he applied the same passion and intensity to his business venture that he had applied to sports, he would achieve the success he had seen in that arena. Besides, he could always rationalize that all it would take is just a little focused effort and he would have his body and health back in no time. It had always responded for him in the past with just a little effort and fine-tuning of his diet.

So work took precedence over building and maintaining his physical body. This went on for months, and the months turned into years. He kept rationalizing about how much it would take for him to come back, or about how he looked in the mirror. He would say things like, "Well, I'm not that bad. If I just turn this way, you can actually still see some muscles under there. This is going to be just a matter of a few weeks of focus. I still got it! Besides, I'm not as bad as that guy I saw the other day. Now, he was really overweight! I will never let it get that bad!"

As the months and years went on, he got more creative with the stories and rationalizations he told himself. In order to relieve the mental stress and guilt from looking at this body, which was in a steady decline, he began to ratchet down his previous standards for health. What was totally unacceptable in the past had now become allowable and judged as the new temporary normal. He began to use the age justification, the old "I am too busy right now, but I will get to it" rationale and the "It's top priority just as soon as I hit this new benchmark in my business" excuse.

As his business grew, so did he. He got even better at telling himself stories that justified sacrificing his health in the short term so he could eventually have all the time in the world to regain the body he once had. The problem was that time never allowed him to implement his plan. There never seemed to be enough hours in the day to get that much-needed physical release of his pent-up energy. It just got easier to make excuses and postpone putting a workout in his schedule. Eventually, he ballooned up to where he was flirting between thirty and thirty-five pounds overweight.

A quick recovery of his body in response to exercise seemed much harder to activate. He was increasingly tired and lethargic, and his brain just didn't operate at peak efficiency as it once did. He knew he was in trouble, but, again, the stories he told himself made the reality of his situation tolerable and enduring. Despite needing to once again purchase a new wardrobe to match his growing physique, he found that he was on life's proverbial treadmill (rather than a literal one) and nothing seemed to stop its endless motion. He eventually avoided the weight scale and his physician because he didn't want to see or hear the truth. His state of health became a mental anchor, weighing down his psyche and affecting the other areas of his health. He began to feel less attractive to his partner, and he began to lose the eye of the tiger he once had. This is the same eye that allowed him to dream bigger dreams and to see possibilities for the future of his personal and business life. He began to realize that a depletion in his physical essence had a profound effect on all his other five essences and, therefore, on his mind, body, and soul.

Deep within you lives a vibrant and passionate soul. You have dreams and desires and a deep need to see them come to fruition. I know you do because we all do. Your eyes, both the inner and outer eyes, are wide open as you take in the possibilities that the world has to offer. At least, it used to be that way when you were a kid. As a child, you knew deep down that anything and everything was possible. The world was your oyster, and all you had to do was believe in your dreams and take the necessary actions with complete vulnerability, and everything would be yours. Read that again and get the two key words in this entire paragraph …VULNERABILITY and ACTION! This means the vulnerability to step out and take massive action without being afraid to confront the negative feedback of the "critics" that are often waiting to become the dream crusher on your journey. The key words "vulnerability" and "action" should signify having unwavering confidence, momentum, and movement.

There's no use having a dream and the passionate desire to get it done if there is no confidence and intention to take action. However, to have confidence and take action, you have to be in consistent forward motion because motion leads to manifestation and manifestation leads to the confidence you need to transmute the ethereal, intangible world of thoughts, dreams, and desires into its physical equivalent in the material world. This is the number-one reason I want to motivate you to be consistent with the care of your physical essence. You have big dreams, and I want you to realize that time is your enemy, so you want to make the most of it and get as much done as possible. To accomplish this, it's essential that your body functions at the highest level possible. If your dreams are big, hairy, and audacious enough to motivate you to sacrifice your time and energy, then you need to put all the odds in your favor, and the bigger the dream, the more energy it will demand from you. Having a body that is able to deliver for you what and when you need it is having the odds tipped in your favor.

Many people claim they don't have enough time for themselves and their bodies, but it's uncanny how, every time my clients come to me in pain or some other kind of breakdown when the body starts to fail them, time all of a sudden becomes the one commodity that they seem to have in abundance, just to regain good health. When pain and dysfunction strike, nothing else seems to matter, as your priorities shift to what matters most. At this point, most people will do anything to get back to their level of health when they were able to fervently attack their daily task list. This is the point when they wish they would have just taken time to care for their body instead of allowing the constant neglect and deferral of their health and wellness plan, if they even have one.

This chapter is not about some specific fitness regimen or a bunch of step-by-step, "get ripped in just six weeks with very little effort" guidelines. Instead, the goal of this chapter is to get into your mind so we can shift your paradigm, your belief system about what having a body in peak performance condition really means for you in the big scheme of things. By now, many of you may be thinking that you do know what having a body in peak performance condition means to you, but the way I look at things is that when someone truly knows something, it shows up in that person's actions and, therefore, the results in his or her life.

We can know something on an intellectual level, but it's when you consistently apply that knowledge even when the motivation leaves you that you really know it on a deep level. I've been in the fitness and peak performance world for over three decades now. I've coached, trained, and guided many people on how to become winners in their specific area of focus. The number-one key to making permanent changes and taking consistent action toward your fitness goals, as well as building up your physical essence, is to shift your mindset and find your "why." Finding your reason why you should make your health your number-one focus has to be the foundation of making any significant changes in your life.

This is why so many people fall into the trap of the "New Year's Resolution Syndrome." As you can probably guess, and I am sure that a large percentage of us have been caught in this syndrome, the New Year's resolution is a phenomenon in which we get caught up in the idea that this is the year that we are going to finally change our lives and reclaim the body and level of fitness that we had in high school. We're going to use the momentum and motivation of a brand new year to clean our slates and erase all the past excuses and lack of consistent action. No more laziness, no more berating ourselves. This is it—a new beginning—and there's nothing like the changing of a calendar year or a change in seasons to help motivate us to finally just do it!

So now, we decide to finally pull over to that gym we've been bypassing each day along our route to work. We envision that all we need is to be in the right environment and around a room of motivated people with the same common goal of losing weight and becoming trim and fit, and that will be all the motivation needed to make the change toward better health and fitness. In this moment of strength and conviction, we also agree to the Cadillac of fitness plans. You know, the personal trainer, the diet, new workout gear—basically the whole nine yards. Hey, if we're going to do this thing, we may as well go big or go home, right? Now, we're set for success. There's no stopping this train now! It's all the way to your destination of a smaller waistline, shapely chest and arms, and tight buttocks. We can just see the end as we envision the feedback from friends and family and the look on people's faces as they witness what total commitment can do. We're 100 percent, no, wait, 1,000 percent motivated! Let's do this!

Then, after a couple of weeks of pain, muscle soreness, and fatigue, plus the fact that our scales just don't seem to be moving as fast as we think they should be by now, our level of motivation begins to wane and the excuses become even more creative as we begin to rationalize why tomorrow or next week would be an even better time to start again. These are all signs that we're beginning to lower our standards to a level that reduces the guilt often associated with the feeling that we've failed to deliver on our goal yet again. This is when it starts to spill over into the emotional cycle of guilt and shame, which further perpetuates the downward slide.

The Physical Essence

The physical essence is about having the mindset that caring for and nurturing this physical body of ours should be of utmost importance. We need to realize that this body is the only means we have to transmute our inner passions and creativity, to tell our own story, play our own music, and dance our own choreography. Yes, yes, yes, we could do all this caring and nurturing of our bodies and unexpectedly get hit by a car while crossing the street; yes, we've all heard of that person who died while running a marathon; but what if you don't meet with such an end, and you actually live to be seventy, eighty, or ninety? What quality of life do you want then? The most precious and reflective times in your lifespan are when you realize the compound effects of your actions. This is very similar to having enough discipline early in life to start consistently adding to your RSP or 401K in order to reap the long-term benefits in your later years; the steady, consistent sacrifice and small, seemingly insignificant deposits start to finally pay off. I think you get the picture by now—it's all about having your "why" in clear view, being disciplined about consistently taking action and delaying instant gratification.

I recently had a client who was now going between a walker and a wheelchair. He had suffered a stroke, which left him with right-sided paralysis of his upper and lower extremities. His speech was also affected, and he was not the sharp-thinking and quick-witted guy he used to be. He was just sixty-two years young and had a whole life ahead of him. He admitted that he lived pretty harshly for many years before the stroke, smoking and drinking quite heavily and never giving a care for what he put in his mouth. He figured that he had to live life in the present moment and let the chips fall where they may. Like many from his era, there was a strong social influence in which our contemporary belief system around drinking and smoking were quite different, and the concerns about the ramifications of one's social habits and vices were not as talked about or publicized. The sad part is that when you see these individuals now, as their quality of life is severely limited, you can see the bitterness and regret as they endure the errors of their previous belief systems.

The problem for my client was that the consequences of his lifestyle choices seemed far in the distance, and besides, he once thought, by the time that anything happened he would be far too old to care, so what did it matter if he took his chances and rolled the dice with his health? Everyone has to die anyway; may as well have some fun with his life and live in the moment, right? Plus, the common rebuttal to the healthy lifestyle argument was always the story of the healthy woman or man who still ended up dying of a heart attack or cancer, so what's the use? Just live for now!

The issue with this kind of thinking is that those who uphold this argument often forget that you will not have the same mindset when you are older, as your thoughts inevitably begin to focus not so much on the quantity of your life as on the quality of your life. In the moment, you may not think long term and consider the future joys of grandchildren, the vacations to your "bucket-list" destinations, chasing your secret passions, or just a day of walking the golf course for a four-hour, eighteen-hole game in the beautiful sunshine.

The average human being tends to be myopic, or shortsighted, when it comes to the ramifications of our behaviors. The problem is that we often think about our behaviors in the moment. Any other outcome seems far in the distance, as we tend to have an affinity for instant gratification instead of long-term delayed rewards. We tend to think that if anything were to happen to us because of our behavior and lifestyle choices, it's that our final outcome will be sudden and painless. So we tend to wager on the risk-reward ratio, erring on the side of continuing to feed our vices. We rarely entertain the scenario that we could actually end our years suffering and in pain. We rarely think how we could have many years left to go with our bucket list unchecked, vacation spots yet unvisited, and grandchildren still to enjoy, but, now, we're missing one key component, a healthy body to help us get it all done!

However, let's not leave it there—the picture can be much brighter, and we can put the odds in our favor. The magic of being human, and our body being as resilient as it is, is that we can change our course in an instant; we can shift the current progression of our health with just some small changes in our beliefs about what being healthy truly means to us in the long term. We just need to move from the mindset of instant gratification to one of a compounding interest and long-term payoff. It's all a matter of educating and empowering ourselves, as well as adopting a different mindset when it comes to our long-term health.

The Magic of Being Human

Here is the double-edged sword about being human and possessing an amazing organism such as the human body: we have an exceptionally efficient capacity to heal, and our bodies are extremely resilient in recovering from the stresses we put them under. Why is this a double-edged sword? Because, due to that resiliency, we often take it for granted, with the expectancy that, with little care, it will always be there for us time and time again. And it usually is. Only when it starts to falter do we decide to make the necessary changes to help it perform in optimal ranges.

Through my extensive research of the anatomy and physiology of the human body, I have summed it all up into one conclusion, and that conclusion is that the human body was built for just one thing—survival! Any other needs, wants, and desires come from the ego and mental and spiritual essences, but, when it gets down to the bare essentials, survival and procreation are the two common denominators. I see it this way: since we exist and judge our reality based on what we experience in the physical and material planes—i.e., we use our five senses to tell us what's "real" in the physical world—then, the physical body is simply the vehicle used to house the mind and spirit and to transmute the intangible energy of the thoughts and desires of those two essences into its material equivalent so it can be expressed in the world we live in. In a nutshell, most, if not all, of us live and judge all that we experience through the physical reality, but we delete so much other information that we fail to comprehend that there's more than the eyes allow us to see.

When you dig deeper into the inner workings of human anatomy and physiology, you begin to realize that what was left up to us to do in order to maintain and promote life are really the basic, menial functions: find food and drink, decide whether to choose fight or flight, and procure a suitable mate in order to extend the genetic code. Everything else—all the myriad of important functions that really keep us alive and well—are an automated, automatic, and pre-wired process occurring under our radar and below our consciousness.

A Well-Thought-Out Plan

So many times, I hear my clients tell me of their pains and aches and what they believe to be their body's functional breakdown. They are often surprised that their body seems to be failing them. The mindset is that their body was never supposed to fail, no matter what it was exposed to and what stresses it was put through over many decades of consistent and constant abuse. What we need is a paradigm shift. We need to reframe how we're looking at the function of our bodies so we can realize that when the body fails, it fails because we've ignored its early warning systems that have been installed to help us in our quest for survival and evolution. We often miss the key signals that warn us of impending danger because we are typically checked out and disconnected from the neck down due to a constant bombardment of negative installations into our mental and emotional essences.

I often give my clients the metaphor of the "check engine" light in our cars; when the light comes on, it tells us something is wrong, not what's wrong. The check engine light gives us a signal that something is going off track within the system and it's time to take it in for a checkup. The irony is that most of us pay attention and respond to the signals for our cars much more intently than we do for our bodies. When our body's check engine light goes on, most of us think that it must just be an error in the system and there's no need to pay attention. After all, the body has never failed to fix the problem in the past, so why pay attention now? Let's keep running at redline for a little while longer so we can see if this is real or just a little glitch in the system. Before you know it, a little problem becomes a big and expensive issue with far-reaching effects beyond the original cause. I guess it's the old saying that familiarity breeds contempt. We become so used to the body's amazing capacity to always be there for us that we build contempt for it as we start to ignore its symptoms and make its needs and desires for attention second place. However, let me take just a few minutes to remind you of the magic of us! Let me bring your attention to the wonders of your physical essence and sell you on why you should do what you can to nourish your physical essence so you can achieve your personal greatness.

Right now, as you read this, your body is under constant assault from the outside and inside environments. Invisible to the naked eye, a constant barrage of bacteria, viruses, free radicals, and various rogue cells are constantly fighting to take over the host and wreak havoc on our overall system. However, in the background and underneath it all, working tirelessly and unrelenting, is a whole system of protective, armed guards, ready to go into battle to save the entire organism. If the body has what it needs—good food with the right nutrient density, sufficient rest in order to recover and heal, an appropriate stress load, adequate exercise and movement, and proper self-care—the body can then do what it does best by promoting long-term health and overall well-being.

However, that is not the case in most scenarios. What is more common is the opposite: food that is deficient of the proper nutrients, too little sleep to recover and maintain balance, an inordinate amount of negative stress, a sedentary lifestyle at work and at home, and a failure to utilize our extended health care package at work to gather a team of professionals to take care of our bodies. It's a wonder why we are so confused and bewildered when the body begins to break down and get sick. We've completely put the odds against ourselves and somehow hope that the body continues to come back time and time again. When you consider how many times it has done its job in our favor, you should be excited about being born into such an amazing creation.

Here's the amazing thing about our bodies: no matter what has happened in the past, no matter how much you have ignored the body and its warning signals and error messages, you can have a second chance to put the odds back in your favor. It's never too late to start now! Our Creator must have known that we needed a vehicle to house the spirit that would be as resilient as possible, one that we could abuse for many decades but would still have the capacity to heal and return as close as possible to optimal levels in order to promote longevity and survival of the species through generations. Let me give you an example of the resiliency of the human body: a red blood cell regenerates every 120 days; our entire skeleton can regenerate in ninety days; our brain cells and body tissues can regenerate in sixty days; our bladder regenerates and turns itself over in about forty-nine days; the liver turns over in forty-five days; we replace the lining to the stomach in about three to five days, and it's even possible to get what can seem like an entirely new stomach in about ninety days; the skin replaces itself in thirty days; the lungs can regenerate after five years of being exposed to a constant barrage of smoke and corrosive inhalants; your bones can regenerate after injury, your brain is plastic and can change to adapt to new experiences and injury; and the list goes on and on. How incredible, wouldn't you agree?

When you think about the constant turnover of our entire body in such relatively short periods, shouldn't the word "resilient" be synonymous with the human body? What if somewhere during this constant and never-ending turnover, remembering that the body has the wisdom and genetic information for perfection, we were to get out of our own way and just give the body exactly what it needs to completely regenerate and restore itself? What do you suppose the possibilities are that come from having yourself a new body within a year to five years of previous abuse? My guess is that we would be astounded at the magic that lies just beneath our skin. Your body vibrates with a constant flow of energy and regenerative activity. At any time in our lives, we are no different than the caterpillar that awaits its transformation to the butterfly that will eventually become free to spread its wings and fly. Where you are now is by no means where you have to remain or end your journey.

Being mindful of your physical essence is not only about working out to keep your body fit and trim, but it's also about proper self-care and maintenance of the physical body. As one of my primary roles is that of a manual practitioner in the healing arts, I would be remiss if I didn't share with you the value of having regular soft tissue tune-ups, energy balancing, and structural maintenance. Here are the "Coles Notes," or summary, on this topic of overall body balance and tune-ups: Every single second of the day, gravity does its job on our body. The constant but subtle pressure of gravity is our greatest enemy when it comes to the wear and tear we experience throughout our lives from birth to death. In order to mitigate the negative effects of gravity, maintaining an optimal posture is essential.

The more our structure moves away from its center of gravity, the more we expose our bodies to the stress, pressure, and tension that gravity can exert on us. With our present lifestyle of being more and more sedentary, it's no wonder that postural imbalances, weakened muscles, chronic tension, and sore and tired muscles and joints are the common complaints of many of the clients who show up to my office each day. Since the human body's natural affinity is to movement, most of our current lifestyle patterns go against our natural design, and this is a setup for a whole host of musculoskeletal strains, sprains, tightnesses, and imbalances. Most of the acute and chronic muscle and joint issues we struggle with on a daily basis can easily be prevented or alleviated with an effective and consistent health and wellness plan. This plan should involve regular intervals of activities that allow movement, stretching, and breathing, in order for our muscles and joints to be liberated, to take them through their natural ranges of motion and to allow adequate perfusion of the body's tissues.

So why don't we choose to work out and keep our bodies at the ready to help us tap into every opportunity to become our greatest selves? This is the big question that I would like to explore in the next few paragraphs.

Why Don't We Consistently Keep Our Bodies in the Best Shape of Our Lives?

If we inherently know that we should move in order to stay healthy, lean, and fit, why don't we? That is the big question that has the researchers and health professionals scratching their heads. The fitness industry is a multi-billion-dollar category, with a myriad of new exercise routines and the latest workout regimens ready to make you fit by simply bouncing, skipping, stretching, and dancing your way to a healthy, lean, and sexy body in just sixty days or fewer! The depictions of those few individuals who were disciplined enough to do the program and the diet for the required amount of time are the hooks that capture the imagination of the primed TV-viewing audience. However, for most of us, the video or the revolutionary new workout never really gets the required time to see the promised results because we soon become bored and distracted as our mental and emotional stimulation wanes and we lose focus on the reason for our initial purchase. The same phenomenon applies to the annual gym membership we purchase with the hopes that this year will be the year we turn it all around.

The problem has been increasing since the advent of the industrial and, especially, the computer age. Human beings are by nature social beings, so getting out and about to socialize was a great reason to also get us moving and connecting within our social circle, but, with the power and far-reaching effects of the Internet, we now have even more reason to become increasingly sedentary as the decades pass us by. We often spend most of our workday on a computer, only to punch the clock so we can head home to socialize for hours with our laptop or digital device in front of us. Our isolation and increasing inactivity is compounding as our reliance on social media increases. We've become addicted to our smartphone devices. Why would we need to travel all the way across town or down two blocks to see our friends and relatives when we can simply check their statuses for an update? We may as well just head home so we can surf and creep the walls of our "friends" to get some mental stimulation and escape from our day of stress and tension at work.

Our inactivity and sedentary lifestyles have led to a problem of epidemic proportions. According to the World Health Organization, worldwide obesity rates have doubled since 1980, and there are now estimated to be more than 1.4 billion adults twenty or older who are considered overweight, and, out of this number, over 200 million men and nearly 300 million women are considered obese. The numbers are also alarming when it comes to our kids; since 2012, more than 40 million children under the age of five were documented as being overweight or obese. In North America, the Harvard School of Public Health reported that two out of three, or 69 percent, of US adults are considered overweight or obese. If these rates continue to rise without some kind of intervention, then the numbers we can expect by 2030 will indicate that roughly half the men and women in North America will be obese.

In order to summarize the insidious effects of our current health and wellness plan, science has coined a term to describe the cost of our inactivity, sedentary lifestyle, and stress. That term, first put forth by McEwan and Stellar in 1993, is *allostatic load*, which McEwan and Stellar described as "the physiological consequences of chronic exposure to fluctuating or heightened neural or neuroendocrine response that results from repeated or chronic stress." So as we continue with our lifestyle of neglect and increasing amounts of stress without any sort of effective physical outlet, the allostatic load of the body begins to mount, and the body is only able to take so much before eventual breakdown begins to occur.

Where Did We Go Wrong?

When I first enter a coaching relationship with my clients, my initial job is to find out what they want and what their self-imposed, limiting beliefs that stop them from getting exactly what they want are. These beliefs affect the strategies they are using to run their daily programming. What is the map they're using to get around the world? Your map, or strategy, dictates and affects every decision you make in your life. We develop these maps both consciously and unconsciously from our early years. These maps, much like the concept of the schemas discussed in the chapter on our emotional essence, lie dormant and under our awareness, wreaking their effect in a subtle but powerful way. As we move forward, let me suggest a few of our hidden roadblocks that limit us from choosing to be fit over being fat and the greatness habits to overcome them.

Greatness Habit #1: Develop a Powerful "WHY"

So what is the real reason most of us choose being fat over fit? The issue is not that we need another new and improved workout program. The problem is that we've lost our "WHY" for getting and keeping physically fit and healthy. If your *why* is big enough, then the *how* will be automatic. The vehicle you use to get yourself in shape is not the main issue; it's the motivation to get it done on a consistent basis that is the key to success. Your reason to work out consistently will be tied to your values. Your values represent your proverbial line in the sand. They give you the internal reason that makes you persist long after the initial motivation has left you. If you think about something you do easily and effortlessly, then behind that will be your values driving it. For example, why do you go to work five days per week for at least forty-eight to fifty weeks per year despite sometimes not feeling it? Well, backing your consistency in this area is a value that says you have the integrity to fulfill your commitment to pay for the lifestyle you created. Or maybe you're driven to avoid the shame and guilt associated with having debt. Whatever it is, your consistent ability to show up and do what's necessary is all about your values and your reason why!

Have you ever noticed how some things seem harder than others to execute, while some activities you complete without a thought? Well, it's all about how the task fits into your values and beliefs. If you can tie your values to the activity, then your success will be certain. Let's take the case of integrating a consistent workout schedule when you have been struggling for years, but you seem to do anything and everything for your friends and family without a hitch and at the drop of a dime. This is because you tie love and connection to your actions as two of your top values and stopping for a workout would distract you from fulfilling your values. The trick to this is to tie the same values of love and connection to the results you'll get from being fit and strong for your friends and family. Being fit through a consistent workout can lead to a longer lifespan to enjoy years of helping and giving. You can also tie working out to the fact that a fit and healthy lifestyle will be a motivation for your friends and family to adopt the same lifestyle, enabling them to be around much longer and able to engage in a healthy and happy lifestyle.

So what are your values? Included in Appendix A is a list of fifty values that you can review; choose the ones that resonate with you most. This is not an extensive list, so fill in any other values that immediately come to mind for you. Follow the instructions on how to narrow down your top five values, and then identify your number-one value that drives almost every decision you make, whether to take action or stay in paralysis. As a side note, remember that your values should also be constantly evaluated to ensure that they are working at the appropriate time and for the appropriate reason. Sometimes your deep-driving values can have a way of working against you. Maybe you are someone who values family; many times, this deep connection to family causes you to suffer from too much guilt and shame as you constantly measure up against a high standard of parenting or being a partner that seems reachable, or you may even find that you pass up amazing opportunities to advance because you stress and worry that it may affect your family life, never giving the opportunity a chance to develop. In the case of the physical essence, your need to put family first may limit you from choosing to work out and join a class because you feel guilt and selfishness over taking this time for yourself.

Greatness Habit #2: Being Consistent Pays Off

We often get this confused, as we think that if we change our workout regimen to the latest and greatest fitness fad workout, then the motivation to keep at it will also stay with us. Variety is the spice of life, right? This is all well and good, but, if you look deeply at those people who constantly look like they are in the greatest shape of their lives and are successfully and consistently engaged in their fitness and wellness plan, without fail, you will find that their level of consistency, repetition, and sameness is absolutely ridiculous. Except for a little variation of the same routine, for years these people will pretty much run like a machine when it comes to being consistent with the workouts they've found to be ideal for keeping their bodies lean, trim, and powerful. It could be golf; resistance exercises such as lifting weights; movement and stretching exercises such as yoga and Pilates; movement and stretching activities such as dance and aerobics; it really doesn't matter—it's really about whatever turns you on and gets you excited on a consistent basis for many years to come. Those who end up failing are those people who find the next new bandwagon to jump on, usually within thirty to sixty days of starting the old one.

The ability to maintain a consistent and predictable fitness routine goes back to the concept that many successful athletes and professionals utilize, and that is that in order to maintain your willpower to do something over and over again on a consistent basis, such as your daily workout schedule, the brain needs to preserve its limited storehouse of willpower. In order for us to preserve the brain's storehouse of willpower and energy for something we want to do, we must reduce the amount of choices we make throughout our day. The more choices we're faced with each day that require us to make more decisions, the more our brain becomes drained of its limited supply of energy and willpower. By eliminating the work of thinking about your workout routine and what needs to be done, or trying to find the coordination and memory for a new workout routine, you make it much easier to commit and go to that class or to the gym for your daily dose of energy boost. By making your workout routine predictable and consistent each day, you will most likely have the willpower to get to it and therefore finally be able to achieve success.

Greatness Habit #3: Fake It till You Make It

Have you ever been in a state where you were passionate about getting your body back in shape? You know, the state of mind where you're just sick and tired of being sick and tired? Maybe it was following a health scare, or maybe a doctor's visit where you got a stern warning about the state of your health, or maybe it was after being motivated and inspired by some event you attended or someone you saw that through many obstacles achieved his or her own fitness goal. Whatever the scenario was, it left you completely inspired to make a change.

So here is one of the primary roadblocks to our ability to commit and remain consistent with our health and fitness goals; it's something psychologists refer to as *cognitive dissonance*, and *Merriam-Webster's Online Dictionary* describes it as a psychological conflict resulting from incongruous beliefs and attitudes held simultaneously. Applied to our context and simply stated, it's when you know that you desire to do something, you can feel it and intellectually you know it's the right thing to do, but your consistent actions, thoughts, and deeply ingrained feelings are completely opposite to the change you desire. Basically, there's a strong disconnect that often leads to recurring frustration.

So what to do in order to correct course and reduce the effect of cognitive dissonance? The goal here is to use the power of visualization to see yourself as you want to be in the near and distant future. With repeated sessions of visualization, you will train your brain to become comfortable and familiar with seeing yourself as you want to be. Even if at first you don't really buy into the vision 100 percent in the present moment. It's the old idea of "faking it 'til you make it!" This exercise is even more effective when you can include all of your five senses in your visualization sessions and imagine them from a real-time perspective—that is, rather than observing yourself from outside in the act of achieving your goal, visualize what you would see if you were actually doing it, as real-time action. It becomes more personal; in neurolinguistic programming, they call this being associated rather than dissociated. This is a very powerful technique used by many successful athletes, celebrities, and professionals!

Greatness Habit #4:
The KISS—Keep It So Simple

I want you to stop and give some thought to your resistance when it comes to connecting with your fitness goal and working on your physical essence. When you picture what you need to do, what do you envision? Do you envision a ridiculous amount of steps that makes execution seem impossible and arduous? Does working out mean you have to go through a battery of preparation even before you hit the gym? Here's what I found is the main difference between those who make working out a consistent habit and those who struggle to even get it started. It's all about how you chunk it in your mind. People who could not go a day without working out and prioritize it ahead of rest and relaxation have a different picture than those who delay or even avoid working out. Those who work out and love it keep it simple with just a few steps to getting the job done, while those who have an avoidance to working out create a multitude of steps before they even begin.

I've conducted my own impromptu experiment by asking my professional fitness clients what makes them absolutely love the grind and what makes them just get it done. I also asked my sedentary clients what makes them resist the grind and avoid taking care of their bodies. Ultimately, the issue comes back to how each group envisioned what it would take to get it done. One side, my fitness fanatics, pictures one or two steps to working out and attacking the grind, and the other group, my sedentary folks, imagines a number of laborious and burdensome steps to getting started. So the goal for beginning and being consistent is all about removing the roadblocks by reducing the number of steps that it takes to commit to consistent action. When people look forward to what they are about to do, in their minds, they construct only a few steps to getting to the fun of the activity. No one likes a whole bunch of steps to getting to fun! Whatever it is you want to do, keep it simple and make the barrier to entry and execution seamless and effortless. Create short, simple, and effortless steps to get started, and see yourself to full completion. Prepare, commit, and execute! Now, go, and get it done!

7

Chemical Essence

Janice came to my office with complaints of pain and chronic fatigue throughout her body. She is an executive in the banking industry, and, at the time, she worked more than sixty hours per week; she often found herself skipping meals as she ran through her busy day. She experienced frequent headaches and lower back pain and was about sixty pounds overweight. She also suffered with frequent skin issues and chronic swelling in her lower extremities. The first area of focus was to address her back pain and headaches through working with her structure and overall function. Once those complaints were stabilized, our next focus was to address the imbalances in her nutritional, or chemical, essence. Then, once her symptoms were alleviated, our final goal was to restore her energy by implementing a workout and strengthening routine to boost her physical essence. Well, this was the plan anyway. However, after a few weeks of attempting to administer the treatment plan, we noticed that we had made minimal changes in her symptoms.

Although we saw some improvements, which gave her hope, she continued to experience fatigue, headaches, and low energy. We were making progress but much too slowly. After revisiting the original plan, I decided to ask a few more pertinent questions about her lifestyle and eating habits. It soon became apparent that I had to reorder the plan so her nutrition was the number-one focus. After digging deeper, I found out that she consumed about eight to ten extra-large cups of coffee each day! She also missed meals, drank very little water, and ate way too many simple and complex carbohydrates each day. She followed the standard North American diet: quick hits of short-lasting energy boosts, such as coffee, donuts, bagels, and muffins. It became glaringly apparent why she felt the way she did and suffered from headaches, chronic fatigue, and weight gain. She was on a downward spiral and had no solid plan to break away from it.

After revamping my course of action, I addressed her diet to alleviate and eventually eliminate the effects of her food choices. My first plan of attack was to change her intake of excessive sugars, caffeine, and refined carbohydrates, as well as her habit of skipping meals. I had to educate her on how her food choices and eating practices were defeating her ability to have the energy to perform at peak efficiency and lead her people effectively in her management position at the bank. In addition, when she experienced headaches, she became even more ineffective and irritable with the people at work and at home.

After about six weeks on the program, she started to lose weight and feel more energy. Her weight loss also led to a reduction in the chronic swelling of her lower extremities, which she had experienced on a daily basis. After about six months on the program, she had lost forty pounds and felt hopeful about her life and her future. Her headaches and fatigue also cleared up, and she was able to lead her team more effectively because she felt more in control— not only of her eating habits but of her life in general. She was no longer a victim to food.

The Chemical Essence

Mastering the chemical essence involves shifting your eating habits away from unconsciously eating solely for the pleasure associated with food. The goal is for you to gain a logical and practical understanding of what foods can do for you. This will allow you to harness the inherent power that foods possess to affect your mind, body, and spirit, as well as the effects that food can have on helping you to reach and sustain peak levels of performance, focus, concentration, longevity, and healthy aging. Too many of us have lost a connection with the purpose of why we actually eat. We've become disconnected from the effects that foods have on us because we've checked out from the neck up. When we eat, we tend to be driven by the yearnings of the stomach and the taste buds, foregoing all the signs and symptoms associated with the foods we ingest. The real goal of eating is to unlock the power trapped in our foods.

Admittedly, food and eating should be fun, and it's all good to eat what you want to eat, but I want you to make your food choices with a conscious level of awareness of the ramifications associated with the foods you select, not just because you think you have no choice when it comes to your food selection or it's what you are accustomed to eating out of habit. Nature has so much variety of colors, spices, aromas, textures, and flavors. Why should we spend all our lives with only a handful of choices, especially when those choices have not been good to us?

The goal is to move from mindless eating to a mindful connection to the power and effect of foods, which can be felt once you become attuned to your body's subtle and not so subtle signals. I find that people who tend to overeat don't actually love food; instead, their addiction to food is more of an ongoing battle with their food. They are those same people who are checked out from the neck up when they eat. They eat unconsciously and blow through every signal that tells them to slow down or stop when they are full and satiated. They are literally in a waking trance state; their energy is scattered, and they are unable to choose to have control. They only become reconnected with the world around them long after the damage has been done and they're sifting through the mental and emotional debris of their habitual eating patterns.

To reiterate, the concept of the chemical essence is about shifting the focus of food away from the stomach, mouth, and tongue so you can clean the filter between your brain and body and be attuned to the effects of the foods you eat. When you are able to successfully do this, you will become more aware of your built-in filtering and monitoring system for food intake. You will start to make conscious decisions based on what kinds of foods feel good and resonate with every cell in your body. Ultimately, the foods we ingest have potential energy locked within them, which is released through the breaking down of your foods to their chemical components. After being reduced to their smallest chemical components of amino acids, carbohydrates, and lipids, our foods work to not only feed us but, also, on a cellular level, to heal and regenerate every tissue in our body. With the correct food choices, we will be able to purposefully scavenge every morsel of food so we can unleash its full potential. The goal is to finally use food to our benefit, to have it serve us. We are going to remove the long-standing guilt and shame that is often associated with the process when food becomes our captor and we its slave.

Let's remove the emotional content from our eating patterns. When we do, we can be clear about why we need to eat and how we can use foods to our advantage so we can have all the energy, clarity, supreme health, and longevity we want and need. We will be adding quality as well as quantity to our long and amazing life. Let's also investigate the hidden psychology around our eating habits that is often at the root of our constant inability to choose the right foods to fuel, strengthen, and rejuvenate out bodies. The intention here is to appeal to your rational and emotional minds so the two can work together in order to educate and empower you to finally make healthy food choices by your own volition and your own motivation, as well as remove the constant guilt surrounding food. Basically, let's get your power back!

The Ecosystem and Our Reason for Eating

So why do we eat? Is it just for the pleasure of eating or to connect and socialize with friends and family? Or maybe it's to be used as an emotional pacifier when we're feeling depressed? Intellectually and intuitively, we would probably answer no to all the previous questions for why we eat, but, somehow, on an emotional level, which is where we all live, these are the ways we approach our eating choices. This tends to lead us onto an emotional roller coaster ride and an ensuing lifelong battle in our relationship with our food.

Let's go back to the basics and pull from nature as to why we eat in the first place. As I sit here writing this, in my backyard, I have a clear view of our apple tree, which leads me to think about the magic of nature in its purest sense. Besides providing us with life-sustaining fruits, this tree of mine provides me with an added and extremely important value. My tree and I share a symbiotic relationship, for as I breathe and give out carbon dioxide, through the tree's own respiratory process, I am supplied with the oxygen and clean air I need for survival. This interaction between all humans, animals, and the environment always leaves me thinking of the perfect balance that occurs each and every day within the ecosystem. As a matter of fact, it's so perfect that the magic flies just below our awareness and remains underappreciated in our everyday, busy schedules.

Merriam-Webster's Online Dictionary describes an *ecosystem* as "the complex of a community of organisms and its environment functioning as an ecological unit." OK, so what does this really mean? This means that we can look at this entire planet as a massive ecosystem, all of its components interacting together and intimately connected with the common goal of promoting life to every living creature within the system. We need every single living thing to make this process of life work efficiently. We are all intricately intertwined and interconnected, even down to those annoying little flies we often complain about, questioning their purpose. Completely rid ourselves of them, and somewhere in the system there will be a shift; at first, it will be subtle, but, over time, there will be a compounding effect and then a major and irreversible shift later on. The key point is to focus on our intricate links with each other.

During my university studies in biology, while the professor went on and on about the ecological processes within nature, my mind sometimes wandered to consider a theory I found very interesting and thought would help me explain to my clients why we eat and the benefit of mindful, healthy choices in food. The theory was about energy and the ecosystem; at the basic level, the number-one source of energy to fuel the ecosystem and drive all the processes involved in promoting and maintaining life is derived from the sun's energy, and since energy is never destroyed and is simply recreated in other forms, our number-one goal as humans, then, is to unlock the energy potential of the sun in order to feed and ignite the power that lies dormant in every single cell in our body.

Let's extrapolate on this thought for a second: every human at any age is always looking to tap into the unlimited source of energy that is within nature. Energy to heal and rejuvenate the body and mind; energy to get to that long list of to-dos; and energy to fuel our brains to maximize our focus and concentration. Well, it is possible to do this. However, once we use it all up during our daily activities, we realize there is really only so much to go around and we've got to do what we can to preserve and replenish it. The only way to maximize our energy resources is to get them from nature's source, which is abundant and never ending.

Now, let's zero in on the main point—do you want to tap into that unlimited and abundant supply of energy? Then, it's pretty straightforward: there's no better way to get to it than to eat foods chock full of the sun's converted bundles of energy. Fruits, vegetables, and other plant sources are the primary vehicles for doing this, as they transform the potential energy of the sun into usable energy through the process of photosynthesis. The second way to tap this energetic potential is through the next best option, which is the animal source that eats the plants and vegetables and can also provide us with the added protein we need. In a nutshell, if you choose to eat live foods filled with the sun's energy potential and a high level of nutrient density, you will be in a better position to prolong and increase your own energy levels. On the other hand, consistent consumption of primarily dead foods such as canned, boxed, and processed foods filled with fat, sugar, and salt will get you, in return, dead energy and lethargic cells that end up working against you to promote low energy, ill health, and chronic disease.

Why Don't We Eat for Peak Performance Living?

You don't need a hundred-plus IQ to figure out that we are what we eat. Even the most out-of-tune person can feel the effects of the foods he or she eats; we all just choose to ignore those feelings in order to continue to consume the foods we want and feed our addiction to the excessive levels of salt, sugar, or fat content. So why, then, do we choose to abuse our minds, bodies, and souls with a continuous barrage of foods that do nothing to promote or prolong a healthy life? Well, I am here to throw you a little lifeline by saying that it's not 100 percent your fault. We've been purposefully conditioned and primed to respond to intelligent advertising gimmicks aimed at delivering on the financial bottom line to their investors each year. Millions and even billions of dollars go into finding unique and powerful methods of getting us to buy, buy, buy, and it's working. The Gallup Poll, the Centers for Disease Control and Prevention in the US, and the *National Post* in Canada collectively state that North Americans have become the most obese population in the world with about one third of North Americans classified as obese.

The funny thing is that although there is an abundance of food available and portion sizes have increased dramatically over the past few decades, most North Americans tend to be fed but not adequately nourished to promote health and longevity. To compound the problem, the lower cost of junk and fast foods has made it even easier to choose the unhealthier fare versus the lean and healthy choices. As the economy continues to be a major hot-button issue, where it seems that incomes decrease while our debt load increases, we are in for a tough battle when it comes to selecting healthy foods over the cheaper and more available unhealthy foods.

Not only have the easy access and affordability of less healthy foods become an issue with our unhealthy diets, but there's also a war being waged to infiltrate our subconscious minds. Advertisers long ago figured out that we don't buy what we need; we buy what we want in order to satisfy our need for instant gratification, whether it be for food, clothing, gadgets, or any other little toys we desire. Every single second of the day, as long as we're connected to any sort of communication device or exposed to any sort of marketing and advertising (which is all the time in today's electronic world), we are being influenced to make choices that are often beyond our conscious thought. The secret war is being waged using a whole host of powerful weaponry: colors, sounds, tastes, tactile sensations, and smells—all are used to influence our buying decisions each and every day. It's no wonder that in today's society, the big money goes to geniuses such as the scientists who come up with unique methods of accessing our emotional centers associated with foods, or the marketers and advertisers who connect us with the desire to get it all now; not so many of the available dollars go into funding to preserve and increase the quality of the foods we eat.

Here's a great example of the power of food to influence us—think about a time when you are shopping in the mall, and among the endless hallways of clothing and apparel stores wafts the tantalizing smell of oven-baked, warm, and moist cinnamon buns. Your senses start to tingle as you become helpless to prevent yourself from visualizing the white, creamy topping drizzled over the warm, swirling lines of infused cinnamon that hugs the creases and crevices of the lightly browned cinnamon buns. You can just imagine yourself with a cold glass of milk as the sweet, cinnamon flavor stimulates your tongue and taste buds and, then, ever so slowly, slides down your throat to finally satisfy your deep craving. And a minute before that, you weren't even hungry. Well, that's my fantasy anyway, and I am sure I am not alone in rolling this food pornography in my mind. This scenario is what is often called the "Cinnabon Effect." The Cinnabon company ingeniously thought out of the box by not associating their familiar, signature smell with other varieties of food odors normally present in the standard food courts of malls in North America. We are constantly bombarded and primed by subliminal messages that aim to affect our food choices.

In his brilliant book *Mindless Eating: Why We Eat More Than We Think*, Dr. Brian Wassink sheds light on the reasons we unconsciously make buying decisions and choose to eat certain foods. Through multiple experiments and research studies, he and his team wisely reveal how we are not only influenced to buy certain products but also conditioned to eat far beyond our bodies' internal signals, which typically would give us an indication to stop once we're full. Hidden cues such as plate sizes, cup sizes and shapes, the sights and sounds of our environment, our attention while eating, the labeling of the package, the colors of our food, and conditioning are just some of the reasons why we make our food choices and why we continue to become a society with increasing waistbands and failing health.

Promoting Happiness from Within

Have you ever felt out of control and irrational in your thinking? Or maybe just felt blue without any apparent cause? No matter how much you try at these times, you just can't shake the lingering feeling of sadness and a deep funk that seems to creep from out of nowhere and be beyond your control. You realize that you really have nothing to be sad about and you should be truly grateful for what you have, but, no matter how you try to change your stream of thinking, nothing seems to be effective and your uncontrolled downward slide continues. Is it that you're losing your mind? Are you suffering from depression? Maybe it's a real bad case of SAD—seasonal affective disorder? Or maybe even some need for medical intervention? Well, there's a strong indication that your unexplained moods, when you've tried all the conventional methods, can be related to the health and integrity of your gut.

Through his book *The Second Brain: A Groundbreaking New Understanding of Nervous Disorders of the Stomach and Intestines*, Michael D. Gershon, MD, became famous for his research that shows that 95 percent of the feel-good hormone serotonin is found to be produced in the gut, or more specifically in the walls of the intestines. This is a significant finding because serotonin is the key hormone that has been often implicated in many mood disorders. Drugs issued to treat mood disorders work on the deepest level of nerve transmission of this key hormone. Most drugs prescribed for depression help to boost serotonin so this neurotransmitter is able to efficiently travel across the gap between the nerve endings, keeping our moods and emotions in check and working efficiently.

There are so many people in today's society who struggle with getting themselves out of the doldrums of their day-to-day routines. Client after client continues to report being unable to handle the stressors of daily life, accompanied by an increase in the dispensing of medications to help them get over the hump until they are successfully able to cope with their issues. The difficulty is that most people are rarely able to find the root of their overwhelming feelings of sadness, stress, anxiety, and depression despite being medicated. So what was meant to be a short-term support is now a permanent addition to their daily routine. Many times, this form of treatment can be a never-ending roller coaster—first the ride up from a low-dosage intake, then an increasing and downward drop, which leads to more powerful prescriptions. Then, the issue is even more compounded as many of my clients who try to wean themselves off the drug when necessary find it extremely difficult, if not impossible, without major effort and discomfort.

The gut is also responsible for another hormone that is integral to your moods and your ability to achieve a feeling of balance. Researchers Peuhkuri, Sihvola, and Korpela, in their paper titled "Dietary Factors and Fluctuating Levels of Melatonin," reported that melatonin is a regulator of the immune system; is involved in the sleep-wake cycle and healthy and efficient functioning of the nervous system; is a protective antioxidant; and, like serotonin, acts as a powerful neurotransmitter in carrying messages from the gut to the brain. There are many more functions of melatonin that are being discovered, but the primary goal here is to realize how important it is to have healthy and efficiently functioning intestines in order for you to ultimately achieve balance not only of your chemical essence but of your other essences as well—which is all necessary in order to move out of the trap of mediocrity and toward your true greatness.

Acid-Alkaline Balance

If you have ever had a pool and had to maintain it, you know that it just takes missing a scheduled chemical balancing to remind you how important it is to keep the pH in your pool in a balanced state. Too high or too low of a pH and there will be a noticeable change in the appearance of the water in the pool, as well as the overall health of the water. A balanced chemistry is key to keeping your pool clean and for making it safe for swimming throughout the summer months. Various chemicals have to be used at the right time and in the right amount in order to keep both bacteria and algae under strict control.

I remember one summer when my family and I made the decision to purchase our very first pool. This was a new experience, and we were novices in the pool maintenance routine; for us, with our hectic lifestyle of running our four kids to their numerous summer activities, it became just another thing on our to-do list. We started off with the discipline and care needed to keep the pool at optimal levels, but, over time, as the novelty began to wear thin, we started to get a little slack on our routine; we started to rationalize why missing one or two scheduled maintenance sessions wouldn't be too bad. Then, one summer, we let a couple of scheduled cleaning and maintenance sessions slip, well, maybe more than one or two. However, to our surprise, it didn't take too long before our clean pool with its blue-bottomed container, which always looked so inviting, started to have a noticeable film of green algae all around the sides and edges, and there was also a darkened tint to the clarity of the water. What was once so tempting that it just felt as if it called you in on those hot summer days now became an eyesore and an avoidance. It was now apparent as to why a faithful and rigorous schedule of maintaining our pool was a necessary exercise.

Human beings are no different. Since they say that we are made up of approximately 70 percent water, our body fluids demand that we also keep the pH levels within a strict range in order to achieve and maintain overall health, longevity, and peak performance. You can imagine the turmoil that can occur when we let our routines slip and get complacent with our health and wellness regimens of regular exercise and eating in the optimal zone. We don't have the luxury of letting things go like I did with the pool. Overgrowth of bacteria and contaminants in the body are much more serious than the few weeks of maintenance that it took for me to get my pool back to optimal levels so we could finally enjoy it again. Too many of us have let the novelty of great health wear thin, and, now, the road back is that much more expensive, time-consuming, and just plain difficult.

The Long and Short of Eating Right for Peak Performance

In order to have normal functioning of our body's physiology (i.e., keeping our pool in a state of equilibrium), it's essential that we maintain a balance between the acid and alkali levels of the body's fluids. A balanced acid-alkaline level is essential for optimal function for each of our cells, for the myriad of functions by the enzymes in our body that help to promote and extend our life processes, and for overall energy production for our bodies to operate at peak efficiency. The ideal levels of acids versus alkali in our body fluids would maintain a strict reading between 7.37 and 7.43, which is measured as our pH. If the blood in our arteries falls below a pH of 7.4, we are said to be in a state of acidosis, while a blood pH higher than 7.4 can be described as a state of alkalosis.

So what can maintaining an acid-producing diet do to you in the long run? Well, according to a study done in 2010 by researcher Daniel P. Heil for the *Journal of the International Society of Sports Nutrition*, a typical long-term Western diet containing a regimen of high fat and protein-rich foods has been linked to poor long-term health, increased risks of cardiovascular disease and heart attacks, increased risk of osteoporosis, loss of lean body mass in older adults, as well as increased risk of chronic disease states. Another study by Ian Forrest Robey, published in 2012 by *Nutrition and Metabolism*, has stated a high correlation between an acid-producing diet and an increased risk of cancer. The acidic environment within the spaces between the cells of your body promotes the invasive and metastatic potential of cancer cells. These are two of thousands of pieces of evidence that support adopting a diet that promotes eating more fruits and vegetables in order to create a more alkaline environment for the cells to do their magic and prolong our health.

These studies all show a significant correlation between our health and what we choose to put in our bodies on a regular basis. Our food choices play a crucial role in affecting the pH balance in our body and, therefore, our overall performance. Most of the issues we struggle with in today's fast-paced and hectic society can be linked to our dietary practices. There is a famous quote circulated among geneticists who will often say that "Nature loads the gun, and our environment pulls the trigger." Meaning that we all have a predisposition to certain diseases, but whether we develop them can be related to our culture, our social grouping, and the foods we habitually reach for. The beauty of being human and living in a "free world" is that you have a choice and all it takes is a decision to change your habitual way of eating to one that promotes and supports a long and healthy life.

Sugar: The Silent Killer

Let's take a quick look at one of the most insidious enemies of getting you to your greatness and attempting to achieve balance in your chemical essence. The enemy—SUGAR! Over the past few decades, our love affair with sugar has gone overboard! Although we've introduced some alternate means of getting our sugar fixes by replacing it with artificial sweeteners, those alternatives do come with a price to our health and they don't even seem to be much better at curbing our need for even more sugary goodness. Aspartame, sucralose, saccharin, and acesulfame are just some of the artificial sweeteners we can get to help us stave off our strong desires for sugar. Although artificial sweeteners have been approved for safe use in North America, both by Health Canada and the Food and Drug Administration in the USA, due to my natural intuition and affinity for keeping things simple, as well as my long research on the body's natural biochemistry, the jury is still out on the long-term effects of these synthetic food additives to our nervous and hormonal systems, just to name two. I would rather not be part of a longitudinal study on the effects of long-term use of these chemicals.

When we first think of the pitfalls of eating a diet rich in refined sugars, we often and easily equate those pitfalls to dental cavities, weight gain, and certain conditions such as hypoglycemia and diabetes. However, most of us have not given any thought or concern to the more insidious and covert symptoms of the allergic reactions that often accompany a high-sugar diet. Some of those symptoms include sinusitis, itchy ears and skin, scratchy throat, mood swings, fatigue, inability to focus and concentrate, headaches, constant and recurring colds and sickness, and that debilitating fatigue that seems to be only satisfied by a quick sugar fix during our typical work day. These are the signs and symptoms of an attack on the body's biochemical pathways that go under our radar each and every day.

So how much sugar do we actually need on a daily basis? Well, according to Nancy Appleton, PhD, in her book *Lick the Sugar Habit*, your body only needs the equivalent of two teaspoons of blood sugar at any time to function properly. Anything beyond that begins to affect our biochemistry on a deep level; it starts to throw off certain mineral balance in our bodies, specifically the calcium, magnesium, and phosphorus balance, leading to a whole host of issues ranging from musculoskeletal chronic pain to issues related to the balance and maintenance of our hormones and nervous systems.

Achieving Optimal Balance of the Chemical Essence

Now that we've covered the most common obstacles to achieving balance in the chemical essence, what can we do to turn the ship around and start heading into safer waters and toward our island of paradise? The solution is not always easy and straightforward, and there is no easy fix. Changing your eating habits is really a personal thing, and there's no one magic bullet to getting it done, no one-stop, fix-all remedy. It's up to you to make a conscious commitment to finally become disciplined enough to break the cycle and implement strict routines so you can regain balance in your chemical essence and, therefore, the balance of your mind, body, and soul.

Throughout my decades of study in nutrition, as well as my own struggle with finding what works for me, I have gathered up a few tips, tricks, and strategies that I want to share with you to help you be more empowered about what and why you should eat. Also, I want to help you gain control and become mindful of your food choices and eating habits. There have been so many diets that have come and gone over the last two to three decades that it could make your head spin trying to find the right one for you. Should you choose the Zone diet, South Beach diet, Paleo diet, or should you go vegetarian? Maybe eating right for your blood type is the key? Or maybe you should wait for the next big thing that's coming around the corner as we speak? I am a nutritional consultant, and even I am confused as to what is my best choice. Well, here is my best advice once again; use the KISS principle—KEEP IT SO SIMPLE. Below are some practical tips and strategies to help you do just that. Keep it simple, and this process will be intuitive and fun.

The Slight Edge
and the Compound Effect

The Slight Edge by Jeff Olson and *The Compound Effect* by Darren Hardy are two great books that suggest that we adopt a "slow but sure" approach to making changes in our lives. I figure that it's much like the long-term approach you would take to reaching your retirement goal—slow and steady with incremental deposits into your financial account, then, one day in the future, with consistent, common sense and disciplined actions, BAM! You are there with a nice little nest egg that pays you off right when you need it, right at those times when you are focused on quality of life and have time to spend the way you want, which is when all the discipline, sacrifice, and delayed gratification really yield results. In this case, we're talking about something more important than money; we're talking about your health and longevity. There's no use having more discipline to pad your financial nest egg if you don't have your health to go along with it.

So the compound effect is all about thinking in the distance while focusing on the daily actions and small steppingstones to get you there. It's about keeping it simple and delaying some gratification in lieu of the greater and more advantageous end goal. Anyone who is successful at anything of value in life realizes that it's all about the process and the constant and never-ending improvements, never about the big, walk-off home run. There are very few who get to enjoy that experience, and it's not long lived. The real hall-of-famers play small-ball and keep themselves in the lineup every single game. That's the approach I want you to adopt—start to discover what foods make you feel good inside. I mean beneficial to your mind, body, and soul. Foods should give you energy and not make you feel fatigue a short time after eating them. Your foods should have long-term health benefits so you can put the odds in your favor, and your foods should help you reach your desired and optimal body weight and maintain it. Once you do that, while adding in a little variety along the way, stick to it, and be disciplined and consistent so you can finally remove the guilt and yo-yo mental beating you are possibly doing now and have been doing for all your life. It's all about the slight edge and the compound effect to getting to peak performance health.

Creeping Calories

Much like the concept of the compound effect mentioned earlier, creeping calories are another reminder how just a little neglect can cause you a great deal of stress. The concept is from Brian Wansink in his book *Mindless Eating: Why We Eat More Than We Think.* Wansink reminds us that just ten extra calories a day, which is only one stick of Doublemint gum, can easily add up over one year to cause you to have to move your belt over another hole. You can imagine this kind of neglect over twenty years!

Let me give you an example. A few years ago, I was watching my son play baseball and mindlessly chewing and spitting sunflower seeds, which is almost like a cultural practice in baseball. One day, out of random interest, I decided to take a look at the nutritional information on the label. I was shocked to realize that after consuming about a cupful, I was actually getting in an extra nine hundred calories! Wow! A whopping nine hundred extra calories, and since eating nuts and seeds has been considered a good thing, I had never stopped to consider the consequences of the extra caloric intake on my overall body weight over time. Again, the creeping calories are insidious foes and, if not monitored, will make a huge difference in keeping you out of balance in your chemical essence.

Plan Ahead

There's nothing more powerful than this little nugget: planning ahead! If you leave your goal of improving your nutrition to random luck and a hope and prayer, then you're setting yourself up for failure. The problem is that when you're feeling the pangs of hunger, at that point, your tendency is to eat anything in sight. I often say that roadkill would look tasty if you've left hours between meals and you let your brain sugar drop dramatically. Planning ahead removes the guesswork from eating through choice, and it supports your ability to commit to your goal of eating to improve your health and achieve peak performance. When your brain has less stress from making decisions, your ability to stand firm in the face of temptation rises exponentially. Over my long career of working with some of the most disciplined and committed fitness athletes, this has to be the number-one key to their success. Over the sixteen weeks of preparation for their competitions, these athletes are meticulous with their preparation and planning. I say if success leaves clues, why reinvent the wheel?

Here is my best coaching advice: every night before going to bed—or, better yet, Sundays are best so you can plan your entire week—plan what you're going to eat in order to feel and perform at your best. When you're able to make your choices in a moment of clarity and unemotional decision making, your chances of success increase tremendously.

Have a Cheat Day

So here you are, you've made your plans, and you've been strict and disciplined with your eating regimen. You've been at it seven days a week, and you are seeing success. Good for you, and you do deserve huge kudos! However, you're now feeling the mental strain and tension of holding out, and, now, it feels like deprivation. You begin to feel a sense of resentment, which doesn't help the desired outcome because you start losing focus on the real goal. Eating and meal planning should be a fun and engaging process. The goal is to make this a lifestyle that you can easily continue for years and decades going forward.

Once again, I will steal a few tips from my highly disciplined fitness athletes who make eating right and attaining their goals a regular routine—when they want to grind through a long and arduous sixteen-week preparation period, they regularly implement cheat days! Yes, they allow themselves to cheat on their plans at least one day or even two days a week. Implementing this plan allows them to make the process a more enjoyable and sustainable undertaking. In your weekly planning, you can look ahead to navigate around certain days that you are committed to social situations that make it difficult to stay on your plan. By inserting a cheat day, you are most likely to have a mental break that will allow you to have the discipline you need for the remaining five to six days of the week, and then you're most likely to achieve success.

Summary

You may have noticed that throughout this chapter, there are no mentions of certain types of foods or protocols. My main focus is on giving you the tools to create your own strategy for success. There are many books, videos, and nutrition plans on the market. It's a multi-billion-dollar-per-year business, but North Americans continue to see obesity rates increase each year. This is because the problem is not solely about what to eat and how to eat it, or some special, new and improved system; the issue at the top of the list is knowing "why" you should eat and having a clear and defined outcome of what you want to achieve and how you want to live your life. I called it chemical essence because, at the end of the day, it's all about how foods are broken down to their basic and smallest components in your body and how your body utilizes your food to heal and rejuvenate your mind, body, and soul.

Soul

8

Material Essence

I want to introduce Jacquie. She was a forty-nine-year-old, busy and successful personal assistant to a wealthy executive. She is conscientious, hard-working, creative, and optimistic. Despite not graduating from a post-secondary institution, she worked her way to being a high six-figure earner through diligence and pure tenacity. Her bonuses were a healthy five figures in any given year. She was very proud of her accomplishments, but the main reason she sought my consulting services was that she was unable to take herself to the next level of growth and often struggled to keep her finances in good order despite making more money than she ever thought possible. She was also single and did not have kids due to her dedication to building her foundation in the material essence. She found that she always struggled to maintain a sense of balance and peace within herself.

Following the initial consultation, I found out that most of her financial pressure, as well as her stress, came from frequently giving loans to her family and friends that were never paid back. She felt trepidation in approaching them to broach the issue because most times, it led to confrontations that left her feeling helpless and frustrated. This was a continuous pattern over the years. She felt indebted to them and also struggled with the guilt of earning "more than her share" and more than her friends and family. There was almost some kind of unwritten code that said she was responsible for their survival and their inability to be industrious enough to make a decent living for themselves. She found that on a deep level, she feared she would be alienated and ridiculed for changing because she had now become more successful than they were, and she worried that if she refused their requests, they would feel she turned her back on them. So to avoid the pressure and inherent guilt of her success, their happiness and financial well-being were now her responsibilities as well.

On an unconscious level, she also felt the shame of not being good enough. Since she never graduated from a post-secondary high school program, she always felt she didn't measure up in the eyes of her family, friends, and—most importantly—her internal, self-imposed critic. After some conversation, I discovered that her struggles with staying financially viable were founded on a deep-seated issue with having overabundance and acquiring more money than she was comfortable with having. On the surface, she felt she deserved to be successful; after all, she did work her butt off to get there. However, she just couldn't shake the shame and guilt of having an overabundant reality.

So what might appear to be unfortunate circumstances that led to her constant state of debt were really self-sabotage to bring her self-concept back into alignment with her deeper beliefs about her self-worth. After some introspection, she was fully aware of the ramifications of lending her friends and family money that they would never (and couldn't possibly) pay back. She experienced the same results every time: anger, resentment, and frustration. This was her mediocrity mindset kicking in. It's a shame that she didn't utilize her greatness mindset to shift her state. She could have done this by realizing that her friends and family were her teachers and not her enemies. She had some serious soul-searching to do in order to uncover the underlying issues with her self-worth and feelings of not being good enough to enjoy her abundance and finally keep what she had worked so hard to acquire.

The Material Essence

What is the material essence, and why should it be classified under the heading of the soul? Our relationships in the material world and with material things are not as they first look; on a deep and intimate level, our feeling that we deserve to have what we want in the material reality is actually a reflection of our contentment and acceptance with having it on the level of the soul.

I can remember getting my first high-end car. I had always dreamed of having this kind of car, but, deep down, I thought it was impossible and I wasn't deserving of it. On the surface, I could tell I was going to get it, but I still felt it could never really happen to me. Over the many years since I was first able to drive a car, I've gone through multiple used cars, most of them old beaters that were always on the brink of breaking down. I can remember my first car I ever bought, a 1977 Toyota Corolla. My wife, who was my girlfriend at the time, pooled her money with me, a tidy sum of five hundred dollars, in order to purchase this vehicle from a friend. If you were to lift the carpet on the driver's front side, you would see that this vehicle was way ahead of its time and came with its very own eco-friendly, fuel-saving technology: if necessary, we could easily put our feet through the floor and run the car ourselves. If some of you can remember the Flintstones, then you would agree that we had a throwback from the stone ages. During the winter months, we not only had to scrape frost off the outside of our windows but the inside as well. There was always a constant smell of radiator fluid as it lost its heater core, and the floor would be soaked with fluid as it leaked back into the cabin. Despite all these issues, the car got us from point A to point B, and for that we were proud owners.

From that time, my vehicles never improved much. It was always one junker to the next constantly in disrepair and always breaking down. I frequently said a little prayer before leaving, so I could feel assured that, this time, I would get there without the embarrassment of being once again stuck on the side of the road. And you have to remember; this is before cell phones were invented, so when you were stuck ... you were stuck!

I eventually graduated to vehicles that were somewhat more secure and stable, but they were always used and in need of some repair. Then, when I was about nineteen years old, I went for it! I had just gotten my first real J-O-B: JUST OVER BROKE. I was finally being paid more than my monthly bills, and I thought it was time to take the leap and get a slightly used car from a reputable, brand-name dealership rather than the usual private owner looking to get rid of his headache and pass it on to some poor unassuming sucker. At least I thought I was stepping up my game. Unfortunately, I got my first lesson in buyer's remorse and "caveat emptor"—let the buyer beware. The salesman saw me coming, and since I was braving the big, bad sales professional on my own, my fear came through. I ended up being ripped off. By the time I left the sales office, I paid far too much over the price.

After some deep introspection and meditation on the entire event, I recalled that I had a presupposition that if I bartered or argued with the sales person, he would have quickly declined my application for the loan! Between my low self-concept and mediocrity mindset, I entered his office in a total losing position. I had no clue of how to enter a trade agreement; I went to the proverbial gunfight armed with only a knife, and a very dull one at that.

This important moment in my life led me to formulate the reason for having a weakness in the material essence and to understand how it can manifest in our lives and lead to mediocrity thinking. The real reason I knowingly paid more money than necessary is that I felt that I got what I deserved and I should be happy and grateful that he would allow someone like me to purchase a vehicle that was much newer than I was accustomed to. This is when I realized that commerce and material things affect more than just our physical or material realities. This experience impacted me on a spiritual and soul level as well.

How many times have you heard about the lottery winner, the celebrity, or even the elite athlete who came into a great deal of money quickly but was left penniless in no time flat? There is an interesting, often-repeated statistic that says that 86 percent of elite professional athletes are destitute three years after finishing their careers. I remember seeing Tyrell Owens, a very highly ranked and highly paid football player, in an interview with Dr. Phil. There he was, an eighty-million-dollar athlete squabbling about paying for his responsibilities to his exes and his children. He was dead broke and living with his parents in his old childhood home, hiding out and running from his responsibilities. He was once the golden boy of football but now the pariah of his profession. From eighty million dollars to broke! How could that even have happened?

What happened was that he had an underlying weakness in his material essence and he was stuck in a mediocrity mindset. His self-concept of his level of deservedness was not in sync with his reality of being wealthy and abundant. He had to self-sabotage to align himself with the model he had for himself, which felt more comfortable. This self-sabotage is usually not on a conscious level. Most people would argue that they would never choose to harm themselves financially, instead blaming it all on bad luck, the economy, lack of education, lack of experience, cheating people, the game being set up against them, and all kinds of other creative and seemingly viable excuses. However, at the end of the day, it's all about a hole in the material essence that continues to bleed, making them financially anemic.

At this point, you may be asking: What if there is a legitimate reason for being in an unfortunate financial position? What if your situation was completely out of your control and totally unavoidable? Many of my clients and associates would passionately argue this point, but, when we break it all down and look at the circumstances surrounding the misfortune, it is almost always associated with the individual's lack of focus and attention to details. Even if you were cheated out of your money by some crafty con artist, you forgot to do your due diligence and check them out. Even if the economy is at fault and your industry overall is failing, you missed bigger signs because you were so busy working that you forgot to take a big-picture view of the business environment so you could spot the changes and adapt. It really doesn't matter what the scenario is; you are the common denominator, and when you take your eyes off the goal and stick your head in the sand, then anything is possible. It's a strong indicator that your material essence is showing some weakness and you're slipping into the mediocrity mindset.

I can remember a time back in 2009 when I was faced with multiple financial situations that threatened to completely bankrupt me and my dreams of success. Both my business and personal finances were in a complete mess. I had more month at the end of my money, so to speak, and I could have robbed Peter to give to Paul, but both of these characters were short as well. I got so deep that I found myself unable to sleep at night. It became a heavy weight as the guilt and shame of my situation spilled over into the rest of my life, and I started to blame the world for my circumstances. Admittedly, most of the reasons for my situation did involve people doing things that were not my expectations, and on the surface level, I could use them as the scapegoats, which I did for weeks or even months. On a superficial level, it felt good to vent my anger and frustration by targeting someone else for my misfortune. Doing this helped to disperse my strong sense of guilt and shame, but it did nothing to help my cause. This was the mediocrity mindset at work.

When my circumstances got bad enough, I eventually stepped back and really looked at my entire situation. I started thinking from a greatness mindset instead. What I realized was that this situation, although it involved different characters, seemed to be the very same one I had gone through many times before. The only difference was that I cast a new set of actors and changed the plot a little, but, regardless, I was living the same scenario over and over. This wasn't an outside job; it was really an issue with my self-concept about what I was worth, as well as my warped relationship with my material essence. My circumstances only began to turn around when I investigated the one common denominator—and that was me! When I started to address my weak material essence and get my head out of the sand, and I actually started to look to solutions that were in my control, everything turned around for me. I once again become empowered to find the way out of my self-imposed financial crisis.

Soul and Material Reality

How does money relate to the soul? Isn't it blasphemy and a total contradiction to include money and material things when we're discussing the soul? Here's the real deal about money: money is actually not about a physical thing. Thinking that money is only a physical thing leads to frustration and stress. Money is about a shift in thought to a higher level—greatness thinking and a greatness mindset. Money is about an idea, a level of personal, mental, and spiritual growth and expansion. Money is about shifting your personal paradigm and belief system. It's not about the physical equivalent of money, which we often go to as a default!

Think about this for a second—money in its physical form has always changed over time. If we go back, we will see that, as time went on, money changed its face to match the mindset of the collective consciousness. For example, between 9000 BC and 6000 BC, the form of currency was livestock; from 3000 BC to 2000 BC, the Babylonians started to get into banking and storing all kinds of currency for trading; then, as time moved on, we started transforming money into coins of all types. In China, leather became the hot currency before paper money was invented between 806 and 821 AD and later propagated throughout the world as an easy means to transfer funds. Then, the power shifted, and those who owned land were the wealthiest and most powerful people once again. After that, the industrial age began and steel became the vehicle for money and power. We moved to technology with the advent of the computer age, and today the primary currency is delivering information. All you have to do is look at the net worth of Google and Amazon to confirm that information is really the latest form of money and power.

The primary focus here is for you to make a mental shift. If you're stuck on the physical level of achieving money and material things, then you will always be behind the proverbial eight ball, struggling all your life to catch up and enduring stress and tension whenever the topic of money and material things is raised. This is working from a mediocrity mindset. I now realize what Napoleon Hill meant when he titled his now-famous book, which has been responsible for creating more millionaires and billionaires than any other book, manual, or course since its publication in the early twentieth century. The book is called *Think and Grow Rich*, and the operative word there is THINK. Money is never on a physical plane. In order to support my argument, I want you to consider this point: Have you noticed that in today's society there is no real need to even have the physical paper or coin to make transactions small or large? Many of us never even see the physical equivalent; many transactions are done on an electronic platform without any actual contact with physical money.

So if you find yourself constantly struggling to make ends meet or just to get your fair share, then you have to go deeper and look at your thought process. What mindset are you working from? Do you find that you struggle with a strong feeling of guilt and shame over having money and material things? If I asked you to visualize yourself living an abundant life, do you find that it's difficult to think beyond your present situation and that the picture of yourself with abundance appears fuzzy, unfocused, and far off in the distance? Then, this is the real reason you're not having what you want in the material reality. Your weak material essence is rarely determined by outside circumstances or events, especially in a society where opportunities are abundant and we can express our freedom of choice to a great degree. Abundance is an inside job and on the level of the soul. True abundance is a feeling and an inner knowing. When it comes from the sacred soul-space, then the sky's the limit and all struggles fall to the wayside. This is thinking from the greatness mindset.

Moving from Mediocrity to Greatness: Boosting Your Material Essence

In my role of helping my clients move from a place of mediocrity to their personal greatness, one of my greatest passions is to help my clients boost their material essences and therefore increase their material abundance by discovering their own untapped capacities to help others get more of what they want from life, which is the key to the distribution and circulation of riches. Over the years, and through helping numerous clients, I have found that the core of all their issues comes from an internal struggle not external. The enemy is not outside; it's really deep within, and the internal struggle typically originates from living with mediocre thinking patterns.

Let's address three specific areas in order to move from a mediocrity mindset to the greatness mindset: first, our relationships with money and material things; second, our ideas of what attracting money means and how to do it without the guilt and secret shame often related with overabundance; and third, our realization that money is the byproduct of expressing our unique gifts and talents to their greatest possibilities. When we can align all three factors, we can then express ourselves fully without having to rationalize our blessings and good fortune or be plagued by the very fruits of our own labors. We will finish this chapter with two practical tips and strategies to turn our financial status from mediocrity to long-term greatness.

Let's first attempt to shed some light on the relationship issues surrounding material abundance. Like many people out there, I grew up hearing how much evil money brings with it. You know, if you have too much, someone somewhere must be getting cheated or is suffering because of your greed. For decades, I wrestled with the guilt of wanting abundance in my life. I grew up with the idea that struggling is a sign that you're closer to your Creator, while to have more than you need is a sin, one you will most likely lose your friends and family over. Basically, I felt as if my desire to increase my share would lead to all the suffering in the world (as if my being poor really helps to alleviate anything at all). That was the message that lay deep in my subconscious mind and created the background to all my resistance to expressing my greatness and accepting the rewards that came with it.

What I also failed to realize is that while I was entertaining and giving life to this thought, I was also pushing aside any abundance that came my way. I continually struggled to accept the good things that were coming to me and were actually well deserved. Each time I got ahead of the game, I would find unique ways, mostly unconsciously, to get back to my comfort level of being just above broke each month.

Each time I went through this experience, I found myself berating my performance. After the initial shock and disappointment wore off, I would shake my head as I realized that I had done it again. The thing is that I knew how it would turn out each time, but I blew through all the red lights and warning signals telling me not to proceed. This is when I realized that it was some unconscious wiring that led me to forgo all my rational thoughts and take the side of my irrational mind. The programming was deep and well entrenched—much deeper than my conscious mind could detect.

What I had to do was reprogram my mind from mediocrity to a greatness mindset in order to reach the subconscious mind, which is the root of my unconscious programming surrounding the accumulation of money. I got into a daily ritual of reading my written affirmation at least three times: morning, noon, and just before bed. I also embedded the information through my auditory channels by listening to myself speak into my future and successful self, telling me about the life I want to have in the very near future. This constant repetition paid off as it began to rewire the neural grooves in my brain that were laid during my childhood. I also visualized myself moving from just paying the bills to having more money than I needed to merely survive.

At first, it wasn't easy to get a clear picture of this vision. My vision of having abundance was distant, vague, and fuzzy. It wasn't enough to stir my emotions and get excited about the future and about having and deserving more in my life. However, after some time of practicing and increasing my power to visualize, the picture started to become clearer and closer and it felt more real. I began to also develop the emotions that are the key to changing our paradigms and rewiring our neural networks. It took about sixty days to finally start to become comfortable with the idea of having and deserving more in my life. Now, I can easily say that I not only feel I deserve more, but I actually expect it, and the funny thing is that it usually shows up.

Second, let's discuss the idea of what attracting money means and how to do it without the guilt and secret shame often related with overabundance. It's this simple—provide the world with more value than you're paid for; you will forever be abundant while making the world and the people you serve that much better off because you provided them with a product or service that far exceeds its value. This sounds pretty intuitive and self-evident, doesn't it? But it seems to be a forgotten art and an overlooked principle when doing any kind of business. When I started to adopt this principle, it drastically changed the way I felt about attracting abundance in my life.

Here's what I realized—a simple equation: value = feelings and emotions. Raise someone's quality of feelings and emotions to another level by providing solid value, and the overall worth of the goods or services you give goes up as well. This is the true source for creating an unending and guilt-free stream of money and material things. It's really an uncomplicated equation. If you help more people get what they want, along with a strong feeling of value, then money and material things will be drawn to you in abundant fashion. Whenever you attempt to go against this philosophy, you will soon realize that you weaken your material essence and retreat back into the struggle and strife of making a living. Besides, giving more value is a win-win scenario; it just feels good when you know that the service you provide has made the user's life that much better.

Third, we need to realize that money is the byproduct of expressing our unique gifts and talents to their greatest possibilities. Have you ever been involved in a conversation about how much athletes and celebrities get paid nowadays? Every year, some athlete or celebrity raises the game and gets some ridiculously enlarged salary for doing something that they seem to do without effort. We enter into a heated debate about how astronomically they seem to push the boundaries of what they deserve. Twenty-five million dollars per year to play baseball from March to October, while professions that are crucial to our survival get a tenth of that price. However, here's an even more peculiar observation: even though we complain and deliberate over each year's announcement of their salaries, we still end up buying the tickets to the stadium, paying whatever price is asked for the t-shirts and apparel, and even driving up sales on the opening nights of the major blockbuster movies!

So why do we have such incongruity between what we say with such passion and what we actually do? Here's why—we champion and support those people in society we unconsciously deem as those who have bravely stepped out to shine their lights and express their authenticity. We may complain at the exorbitant rate they receive for their bravery, but, after the initial shock has worn off, we willingly reward them for the expression of their greatness and their ability to be completely vulnerable so the world can enjoy their gifts and talents. The more they are able to become vulnerable by expressing themselves authentically, the higher the levels of income will go, and the more we resist shining our lights and truly giving a piece of our souls to the world, the more struggle we will experience as we attempt to figure out the master key to abundance.

This brings to mind the classic story of the parable of the talents, taken here from Matthew 25:14–30 in the *World English Bible*. The story begins with the departure of a master from his home to faraway lands. Before he leaves home, he gathers his three servants and gives them talents (a large unit of currency) based on their level of ability. The first servant receives five talents, the second servant receives two, and the third servant receives only one. The master leaves on his journey, entrusting his servants to keep his money safe until his return. After returning from his long journey, the master gathers his three servants to have them return his talents. The first servant explains that instead of just keeping the master's talents safe, he took some initiative and, through his efforts, doubled the value of the talents. With that the master says, "Well done, good and faithful servant. You have been faithful over a few things, for that I will set you over many things. You can now enter into the joy of your lord."

Then, the second servant returned with a similar report; he also doubled the talents he was given, and, for that, the master also granted him entrance to the joy of the Lord. Finally, the third servant approached and reported that he had played it safe by hiding the master's talent deep in the ground. The servant proclaimed that he knew that the master was a hard man, reaping where he did not sow and gathering where he did not scatter. He said he was afraid and hid the master's talent in the ground. He was proud to hand the master's talent back to him safe and sound. To his surprise, the master was enraged and punished the servant. He told him:

> You wicked and slothful servant. You knew that I reap where I didn't sow, and gather where I didn't scatter. You ought therefore to have deposited my money with the bankers, and at my return I should have received back my own with interest. Take away therefore the talent from him, and give it to him who has ten talents. For to everyone who has will be given, and he will have abundance, but from him who doesn't have, even that which he has will be taken away. Throw out the unprofitable servant into the outer darkness, where there will be weeping and gnashing of teeth.

Once I read this story, it made a massive effect on my psychology. It helped me to get the big picture as far as expressing my talents and not keeping them hidden safely deep in my soul. In this case, the word "talent" can be translated into its present-day equivalent. Here's my take on the story: from our Creator we were given certain talents. Some of us received many, and some of us were given one specific gift. How we use our talents will dictate how we multiply our riches in our material reality. By investing in our talents and increasing their worth, more will be given to us, in addition to an increase in our expertise and preeminence, which will be our reward.

This brings me to a quote that seems to fit perfectly. Author Leo Buscaglia wrote, "Your talent is God's gift to you. What you do with it is your gift back to God." Amen to that.

Gratitude and the Material Essence

I cannot think of any act more powerful or any act that more facilitates your journey to greatness than having gratitude for what you have and for what is not even here yet. Gratitude opens you up for more goodness and abundance to flow in. Practicing gratitude is not some *woo hoo*, New-Age trick to build yourself a nice place on fantasy island. On a pragmatic and realistic level, regularly practicing being grateful for what you have opens you up to see more of what you want and less of what you don't want. Here is why this is important: the human nervous system was equipped with a sensory system that has been tuned to find dangers in your environment, which means that you are more apt to search for what's wrong in the world around you. So it's your natural tendency to search for negative and dangerous elements in your environment, often deleting the good things in your life and becoming hyper-focused on what's wrong.

As of this writing, it is not difficult to come to the conclusion that the world is in a tumultuous time and space, and with the connection we have to all the options of social media, we are always "informed" about the first hint of bad news. In an instant, we can receive word of natural disasters, social unrest, murder, world tensions, and grotesque and graphic pictures of atrocities being inflicted by acts of terrorism. What used to take days or even weeks to get to us can now be presented instantaneously and repetitively in many different variations as each news delivery service fights for our attention. How easy is it to be positive about life today? Plain and simple, it's not! So in today's society, it becomes that much more difficult to adopt a greatness mindset of gratitude when the world seems as if it is falling apart right around us.

This is a mediocrity mindset and even more reason why we need to implement the practice of being grateful for what we have while we are waiting for the goodness that will certainly come our way. We cannot let the few incidences of bad news, which are constantly looped and squeezed out for more blood and guts and ratings, cause us to become myopic and forget that with over seven billion people on our planet, there are more people looking for peace, love, and solidarity than there are people looking to hurt and maim others. It's just that the extreme behaviors have much more of a dramatic effect and we are drawn to focusing on the few.

Should we stick our heads in the sand and pretend violence doesn't exist? Absolutely not! But what good are you doing if you are paralyzed by fear and simply part of the collective consciousness of pessimism dreading the destruction of the world as we know it? Would it not be a better and more effective plan to keep focused on the good that we can become while taking positive actions to see that end come to fruition? The only thing that can eradicate the darkness we are experiencing right now is to bring our world into the light of optimism and love. It was Albert Einstein who was quoted as saying, "We can't solve problems by using the same kind of thinking we used when we created them."

Raising Your Level of Material Essence – Shifting to a Greatness Mindset

In order to increase the level of your material essence and move to a greatness mindset, you have to become comfortable with the idea of having more than just enough. I often muse at the fact that so many of my clients shy away from their abundance. When asked to claim what they want from life, many develop trepidation at having to proclaim a level of material wealth above their belief of what they think they are worth. We all have a certain comfort level that we think we deserve, and asking someone to even nudge up a few degrees above this predetermined level can lead to a great deal of stress. With my coaching clients, I have found it interesting that an exercise of writing a number that seems to be even an incremental rise above the level they believe is possible will often lead to increased stress and eventual retreat back to their previously self-determined comfort zone. If we can't even get ourselves to secretly entertain an imaginary number without it being a cause of anxiety, then how can we possibly increase our level of material abundance and therefore attain a balanced material essence?

So the first step is to allow yourself to proclaim that you are worthy of limitless abundance and life's unlimited resources. Become comfortable with the fact that you are not doing anyone any favors by limiting your personal growth and potential by being a martyr for some unknown cause. Suffering is not your birthright, and it serves no real purpose to remain in fear while adopting a scarcity mentality. I realized that from where I started in life, I was given an opportunity to raise my game to its highest potential. It would be a travesty to not use that opportunity to grow beyond my present level of consciousness each time. By remaining at the bottom of my potential in order to assume a demure and passive servant role, I am not only harming myself through self-depreca-tion, but I realized that I am doing no good for my family or those that are affected by me either. I realized that when I raise my game, as Maryanne Williamson wrote in her poem "Our Deepest Fear," I am unconsciously giving permission for my circle of influence to raise their game as well. You would not be reading this book right now if I had given in to playing a small game by living and acting from a mediocre mindset.

Practical Tips and Strategies for Long-Term Greatness

The 10-percent rule – save 10 percent of what you earn

I have never heard any better advice than this; it's short, sweet, and straight to the point. Have you ever stopped to think back on all the money you've earned in your working life thus far? What would 10 percent saved give you in liquid cash right now? Never mind add-ing compounding interest at the rate of inflation to that number. Take a minute just to do the simple math of calculating or guess-timating your total net income over your past working years. How much is that? Now, calculate 10 percent of that income, and think about having that at hand when you need it.

The next thing I want you to think about is this—could you have lived on 90 percent of your net income if you had been dis-ciplined enough to alter your lifestyle to allow that to happen? In addition, how much of an alteration would that be for you and your family? Would taking away 10 percent when you first started and putting it into savings have altered the quality of your life that much? How many times have you wished for just a small raise or bonus in pay so you could get out of the situation you were in, only to get that raise or bonus and end up right back where you were in the first place financially? I heard a simple but profound quote from Mark Victor Hansen, co-author of the *Chicken Soup for the Soul* book series: "If your outgo exceeds your income, then your upkeep will be your downfall." How true is that? But, again, that's all an internal job, isn't it?

Now, let's not get too depressed in thinking that you've missed the boat on saving all that lost money. No matter where you are now or how deep you are in debt, this exercise of saving 10 percent will be your life preserver to freedom. All you have to do is start right now. Here's an easy trick to get started, something I started to do using the magic of technology and this simple rule: pay myself first. Using the technology embedded in most large banks all over the world, you can set an automatic withdrawal system that will consistently transfer money from your main account into a separate savings account that you can call your "financial freedom" account. When you set this up to run consistently and treat this habit as you would any other bill payment that must be made each month, you will be amazed at both the amount of money you will save and how many times this consistent habit will pay you back in times of dire need. I adopted this habit after reading a little book called *The Richest Man in Babylon* by George S. Clauson, which is a time-honored classic that still stands true and passes any test of its principles. Start today, and be consistent, and in time you will be thankful you did.

Profits are more valuable than wages — build passive income

This idea has had a massive effect on my thinking and caused me to make some serious paradigm shifts. Jim Rohn, who was an author and modern-day business philosopher, wrote and spoke about this concept, which led me to deep contemplation, meditation, and an eventual "Ah ha" moment when his philosophical statement became clear—profits are more valuable than wages.

Here's the gist of this. During our most influential years, as we began to venture out into the world to blaze our own paths, we were conditioned to think that our best method to financial stability was through seeking a job that would pay us a certain wage with the possibility of increase if we either stayed in the company long enough, continued to upgrade to the required skills, or networked with the right people. This sounds somewhat straightforward until you soon find out that there really are no guarantees to this plan and many times there is the proverbial glass ceiling that stops your upward mobility and limits your potential greatness.

This idea worked for many decades and served its purpose during the industrial age, but, in today's business landscape, there is a more frequent reality—DOWNSIZING! In an instant, your little nest egg that seemed so certain can be taken away with very little notice. So what do you do about this, and how do you avoid this unpredictable outcome? Begin to shift your perspective on making your living from a standpoint of only earning a wage to a standpoint of creating profit.

What are some ideas for making profit? Do you have a training system you would love to create that you can sell or charge an income for as a consultant? Maybe you've had that book idea for years, and you have never taken action on bringing it to reality. Is it time to take the leap and dive into that network marketing opportunity that you find you're passionate about but haven't had the courage to commit to due to the stigma surrounding network marketing? It could even be that start-up business that you've been sitting on but have not taken the time to initiate. You can even consider taking that 10 percent of your wage and giving it over to a great financial advisor to help get you 3 to 9 percent per year of compound interest. It doesn't matter what vehicle you choose; just change your thinking from making a living in the moment to creating a passionate life and going for your greatness by way of a continual and always circulating profit center.

Summary

In summary, attaining balance in your material essence is not just about tirelessly going after money and the trappings of life. It's about being comfortable with your ability to accept what you deserve in life and not carrying the guilt and shame of your rewards for providing value in the world. It's also about moving away from a mediocrity mindset and toward a mindset of greatness. We live in a material reality, it is what it is, and we cannot deny that fact. There is an amazing connection between your ability to accept what you're worth and the peace and contentment you will enjoy on the level of the soul. If you're having trouble connecting soul and material essence, then all you have to do is to imagine how it feels to be in debt and the heavy pressure of living below your potential. It's that feeling when you know you can be, do, and have more, but you limit your potential by thinking that you aren't deserving of such abundance and rewards.

Human beings were meant to shine and continually express themselves to the world at the highest level. If you learn to accept the fruits of your labor without being tethered to a heavy feeling of stress, tension, and shame, then you will be able to continually raise your game and shine your light. When you can do this, you become the beacon that helps to guide so many people out of the darkness of mediocrity, and then the effect of one becomes the reality of many. Once your cup becomes full and begins to overflow, I am absolutely sure the runoff will be more than enough to satisfy the thirst of our society and to quench our parched taste buds with some positivity and hopefulness.

9

Spiritual Essence

Spirituality has so many different meanings in our modern society. When asked about religion, many people are now quick to proclaim, "I am not really religious, but I am more spiritual." What does this really mean? Are they referring to the classic definition of God and religion, or are they part of the growing population that has been disillusioned by the dichotomy often reflected in many religious groups in which followers pray to their God, but, then, their actions and lifestyle display something completely different than what is truly meant by the holy text they claim to follow?

The confusion also lies in the fact that at the root of most of the tensions and suffering we see in the world today is a group who uphold a strong belief in a certain dogmatic religious doctrine. How could we speak of the same loving and kind God while we witness acts that aim to cause harm, breed hate over generations, instigate war, and lead to the separation of people and a struggle for supreme power? It's no wonder that so many people in North America and many parts of the world who stand by and watch the conflicts are now unable to claim their love and devotion to the classic definition of God and religion.

So what exactly is the spiritual essence all about if it isn't about a relationship with a certain god-like figure? Spiritual essence, in this case, is all about our relationship and connection with ourselves. When we speak to ourselves in times of contemplation, whom is it that we speak to? When we have hunches and gut reactions, where are those emanating from? All those thoughts and deep introspective moments we experience all day long—what initiates and propagates those thoughts? When we feel love and passion, what sparks that feeling? Why is it said that when we are moved to act, we feel it down to our souls? And why or where do we have these deep and often-unyielding drives to fulfill our destinies? These are just some of the questions that give us a glimpse of the spiritual essence at work, and when we are able to connect with this essence, no words are needed, as the answers to the above questions seem to become illuminated from deep within.

The goal of this chapter is not to turn you away or even tarnish the strength of your conviction to your particular belief system, but, instead, by understanding and applying the words on these pages, to create a stronger connection to whatever it is that you currently believe. I am a student in this game of life, as you are, but I do know that if I have a greater connection to who I am and a sense of gratitude for what I have been given and what has still to come, then my union to my beliefs will be strengthened even more and I will ultimately move closer to my personal greatness. Since it has been said that we are a reflection and an image of the Creator or universal consciousness, then loving and appreciating what and who we are is a great start to increasing the bond between us and whatever we believe.

In the process of developing this concept of the spiritual essence, I have had a few key experiences that have turned me from a skeptic into a believer that there must be something bigger than us at work in the background, guiding and directing our actions along the way. However, with the increasing pace of today's lifestyle and ever-mounting stress loads, we are hardly ever able to tap into the hidden messages of the universal and collective consciousness. I am an avid believer in the act of journaling my experiences, so I would like to share some of my moments of clarity that have enabled me to not only discover the spiritual essence but also to tap into it on a regular basis in order to gain balance and peace in my life.

Each experience you will read is a chronological step in forming my discovery of the spiritual essence. These experiences, you should note, are also from a microscopic viewpoint to a macroscopic level of awareness. As I progress in my understanding of the spiritual essence, I move from an intangible base of reality to a more tangible way of understanding nature and how being connected spiritually plays a strong role in our lives. What I will cover are just a few specific and poignant examples of my "Ah ha" moments that shed some light on this ubiquitous force of nature called spirit. Of course, there have been many more, but these are the times when it struck me the most that there is an underlying and unexplainable guiding force that we may never be able to objectively validate. I think it was set up that way by purposeful design and intention. There are some times in our lives when we need to trust our gut and intuition, give up the doubt, and just let go. As was said by the Sufi poet Rumi, "We have to give up the drop and become the ocean."

Experience Number One

In 1992, I stumbled into a training program named *Therapeutic Touch*. I say stumbled because at that time I would never have voluntarily chosen to join such a program and be around the types of people I thought would typically sign up. What I mean is that

I only bought into what was within the realm of the norms of the masses and I wanted to stay out of the realm of the fringe health care practitioners. The only reason I ended up in this group is that I mistakenly, in my ignorance at that time, understood "therapy" and "touch" to be some sort of manual therapy, or hands-on-the-body technique. Little did I know that it was all about feeling the energy that surrounds the human body! The worst part was that I signed up and paid for a twelve-week duration, and by the time I realized that this program wasn't for me, the deadline was passed and the fee was non-refundable.

I ended up sticking it out for eleven weeks, and I must say that by the end of it all, I began to actually feel the presence of some kind of energy field between my hands; then, eventually, I extended that to a bigger field around the human body! Although I had this epiphany and new insight, I was still a skeptic but now with an open mind.

Now that I had this awareness of the energy field that emanates from all living things, my mind began to wonder, *What and where does this come from*? I must admit that my skepticism kept me from completely integrating this knowledge into my practice at that time, but, no matter how much I denied it, I kept having this strong feeling that if I didn't at least consider it, I was missing a key part of the puzzle when it comes to improving the quality of my clients' overall health. I think intuitively we all know that there must be some existence of this energy field, but, like me, our skeptical left brains keep us from crossing over to the dark side and drinking the Kool-Aid. Tell me this: If we didn't believe in the existence of some kind of energy, then why would we continue to freely use such phrases as "I just have no energy today"; "I don't like the feel of this person's energy!"; or "He/she just has a certain energy that I resonate with"? I think on a certain level, we have an affinity to this concept, but our conditioning prevents us from going with it completely.

So how does this tie into the spiritual essence and getting to your greatness? Well, here is what I discovered over many years of application of this knowledge with literally thousands of clients: when we are fatigued, depressed, overworked, sick, or injured, strangely, this field of energy downshifts to a lower level of vibration. The longer we stay there, the more we will experience a depletion of our energy, which can then be felt not only by the individuals experiencing the event but also by those around them.

Does this sound a bit far-fetched or kind of esoteric and out there? That's OK; I was there too until I thought about my relationship with someone I was connected to on many levels. For example, consider your partner or spouse, your children, or maybe your closest friend. Now, reflect back on times you have been able to figure out that they were not exactly feeling well and that they may be a bit off their game that day, and this is long before they even knew it. You could just tell that something was wrong and their energy was a little off. You could even experience this from a far distance. We've all heard or even experienced the moments when we had a premonition that someone we love was in need of help or was thinking about us at the same time. That's your intuition at work, your sixth sense and your gut feeling.

After being with someone for a long time, especially when that person is closest to you, as with a mother and her child, you just seem to develop a sixth sense and your communication starts to happen on a whole other level. It's far below what your conscious and rational mind can process. Why do you think we judge everyone we meet by making a "gut" decision about them within the first ten seconds? This is one of those protective mechanisms set up in our nervous systems that helps us to judge whether or not we are in danger. The problem is that we stop actively developing these skills of reading the world around us, defaulting to a mere belief in what the five senses can detect, which is ironic because we are deceived by these senses more often than we know. Why do you think many eyewitnesses that testify in court are dismissed later on?

Developing and strengthening your spiritual essence in order to reach your personal greatness is about raising your levels of energy. They go hand in hand. When your spirit, or soul, feels rejuvenated and invigorated, you radiate a certain kind of energy that is very often visible and, most importantly, palpable to anyone within your circle of influence. As an exercise, I often give my clients who are performers, athletes, and sales persons a process that involves raising their energy by projecting out to the back of the auditorium or within the group they are presenting to, almost as if they were physically stretching and pushing themselves out to fill the room. This is all just an imaginary stretch and push, mind you, but somehow it causes my clients to project outward from within themselves a certain kind of magnetic energy that enables them to increase their levels of performance and influence.

The idea is that we don't watch someone perform with only our eyes and ears. Remember: as Mark Bowden notes in *Winning Body Language: Control the Conversation, Command Attention, and Convey the Right Message—Without Saying a Word*, communication is 93 percent nonverbal; we feel the performance with our whole beings. The goal for my clients in this exercise is to put their energy in every seat of the house so their energy or spirit can be felt and connected to their message. This energy can be very infectious to those within its reach. This may sound touchy-feely to some, but you have to give it a try before you push it aside. Remember: I was once a complete skeptic as well. That's until I started to apply this information with great success. You can try this too if you're faced with a presentation or a meeting at work in order to have maximum effectiveness and influence.

So in summary, my experience with working within the energy field gave me an insight that there is something going on that is below the level of our conscious minds and awareness. I realized that whatever we experience in both our internal and external worlds would also be reflected and integrated in our bodies. If left long enough to become chronic, it will migrate to the deepest level of our being and what we think and feel about our experience will be projected out to the world around us. I continue to investigate and stay open to this strange but real phenomenon, so the story continues to evolve.

Experience Number Two

It was a few years later when I had my next exposure to this concept of the spiritual essence. I had just graduated from a program in massage therapy when I decided to improve my skills by adding another tool to my repertoire. I had heard about the power of a therapeutic modality called *cranio-sacral therapy* (CST). The idea behind CST is that the body has an inherent biodynamic force and rhythm that fluctuates and moves fluids throughout the body in a specific and predictable timing and pattern. This rhythm is separate from the rhythm of the heart, respiration, and other bodily functions. In the classic osteopathic circles, this rhythm is referred to as our *primary respiratory mechanism* (PRM). They call it primary because it is thought of as the key rhythm that sustains and animates life in humans and animals.

Because of my skeptical nature when it comes to adopting and professing that something is gospel, I must be able to rationally explain my beliefs and substantiate my findings. I rarely ever speak on any topic that I'm not fully familiar with or ones that I lack the proper information to entertain a good argument in defense. So despite the investment of my time and finances, I have to admit that it took me a while to completely buy into this philosophy.

The big turning point and "Ah ha" moment for me came when I had a client who turned out to be my greatest frustration and yet became my greatest teacher. We had been working together for some time as we attempted to find her relief for the chronic pain she incurred during a motor vehicle accident. We had gotten her to a certain level of wellness using the traditional approaches, but we hit a plateau about three months into our treatment plan. The process became daunting and frustrating, as she would show up each session with very little improvement. At that time, my skeptical attitude got in the way as I avoided implementing any other treatment modality that seemed "out of the box," so I stuck to the traditional soft tissue therapy, strengthening exercises, and structural balancing. It was because of my frustration that I decided to take a chance and try the new modality, which I kept in my back pocket for all this time. My client agreed to take a leap with me, and we moved ahead.

I began by carefully feeling for the rhythmic pulsation that was supposed to be apparent in every tissue in the body. I had glimpsed this rhythm during training sessions, so I was optimistic about finding it. It took me about ten minutes to tune into the rhythm. It began as a subtle but palpable pulsation just under my hands. I questioned what I felt, but it was so distinct that I could not deny its existence. In and out, ebb and flow, the rhythm went through its cycles, and with each application of the fine-tuning technique, the rhythm and cycle became much clearer and more refined. I kept with it until the prescribed treatment plan was complete; now to wait for the outcome.

Upon her return a few days later, I checked in on her progress, and, lo and behold, to my surprise, she had made an 80-percent improvement. Her sleeping improved, her headaches were relieved, and her pain levels dropped! I was astonished and encouraged to dig deeper into this newfound power to help my clients heal and recover from their long-term aches and pains. The questions were now: What is this rhythm, and what is the answer to why it affects the overall health and wellness of my client in such a profound way?

Over the next few months, I kept at it and continued to train my skills so I could increase my level of touch and fine-tuning. Client after client, I kept feeling more and more. The level of my palpation kept increasing, and I became more certain of what I was feeling while the awareness of this distinct rhythm became more apparent to me. With more experience, I started to find connections to this rhythm and to my clients' overall health and vitality. The better my clients felt about their overall health status, the more vitality I began to feel under my hands; the more my clients reported feelings of ill health and traumatic injuries, the less I was able to feel under my hands. The more they reported being chronically sick, tired, or depressed, the more I felt a correlation to their rhythmic impulses, which were also more muted and less perceptible.

So what was the root of this rhythmic impulse, and how did it help to form the spiritual essence? These burning questions kept me passionate and curious about the discovery of this underlying rhythm within each tissue of the body. My curiosity led me to an in-depth study in a number of areas, including embryology, anatomy, physiology, psychology, philosophy, energy medicine, and some of the information left behind in the old osteopathic manuals. What I found is that within each cell of the body—and I remind you that the body is comprised of trillions of cells—there is a self-governing system that keeps each cell alive and continuously promoting the life of the entire organism.

Each cell performs its own little dance, exchanging fluids and chemical messengers in and out of the cell. Each cell is literally a powerhouse all on its own. It has been said that if you could just harness the power of all the cells in your body and direct them to one focused intention, you could light up a small town for weeks, if not months. This gave me the answer as to why, with some focus and intention, I could pick up this fluctuating impulse of the body. It was a collective and synchronized coalition of all the tissues in concert, and if they were healthy, they would emit a vibrancy and power that could easily promote and sustain the vitality that is necessary for life, but, if they were experiencing a diminution in strength due to external causes, which are usually related to our lifestyles and habits, then they would become infectious. When this happens, we experience a reduction in energy and a loss of our spiritual essences from micro levels to macro levels.

Most of my clients who come to me with a history of cancer, heart disease, multiple sclerosis, or other auto-immune-related conditions usually aren't just sick on a superficial or physical level, as these conditions don't only show up randomly every time; they are usually a case of long-term and consistent dampening of their spiritual essences on a deep level. The constant exposure to stress doesn't just make an impact on the surface. In time, it begins to happen on a deep cellular level, and, if left long enough, it will eventually connect with each cell of the body to cause a long-term and debilitating effect. This may explain why so many of these chronic states become intractable and unresponsive to traditional treatments. In order to treat them, we must work from a truly "whole-istic" viewpoint by addressing the mind, body, and soul.

So once again, each experience of feeling nature's inherent forces, both energetically and within the tissues of the body, enabled me to realize that what we feel and experience in our lives on a thought level most definitely will eventually show up in our bodies in some way. I began to realize that our bodies are just the vehicles that connect our spiritual or thought experiences with our physical and real-world experiences. I realized that every client who walks in my treatment area tells a story within his or her body, and if I am in tune enough, I can read each chapter and page to eventually get to the real story, or primary source of the chief complaint.

Experience Number Three

Now, let's move from a more microscopic view of my experience to something on a more macroscopic level. This story is near and dear to my heart and involves a meaningful time in the lives not only of me but also of my entire family. The year was 2006, and I can remember being home that day when we got the news that my niece, who had been battling all her life with cerebral palsy, had just passed away. She was only fifteen years old, and she didn't live much of a life, always in pain from the excruciating and contorted posture of her spine and ribs. Her pelvis, spine, and head were mis-shaped, twisted, and torsional, and the condition wreaked havoc on her body. It almost looked like she was shrinking from the inside out, as her head and rib cage were concaved with the internal pressure from the living tissue experiencing such stress. Because of the compression of her ribs on her lungs, her breathing was labored and restricted. She had eyes that were converging and never really stayed steady and focused. She was never able to speak and only responded to a familiar repetition of a sound she often enjoyed to hear, as she smiled in response to hearing it. This gave us a few moments to feel like we had connected with her. The cause of her passing was related to the increased pressure of her thorax on her struggling heart. It was ironically almost a bittersweet moment as we all realized that her fight was finally over and there would be no more pain.

When we received the news, we quickly made plans to be there so we could say our goodbyes and lend support to the parents. I was very connected to my niece, as my wife and I often spent a great deal of time with her, which also served to lend support to her parents so they could have some time for themselves. This also allowed us to have a lot of time to experience, to a certain degree, what it must be like to care for someone with this kind of disability.

When we arrived at her home, our hearts collectively beat faster as the reality of the event got more real. As we parked the car and headed toward the house, our minds started to spin, as we weren't certain what we would find. We met her parents, who were actually maintaining some composure during this extremely tough time. I had this awareness that they too were feeling that despite this horrific event, it was also a chance for my niece to finally be at peace.

After meeting with them, we approached with massive trepidation the room in which she lay. It seemed to be the slowest walk I had ever taken. Finally, there she was; emotions came flooding in as it all came to reality that this had really happened. I went from pain, loss, sadness, and remorse to regret and confusion about life itself. What was the meaning of it all? What is our purpose here on earth? What is this journey all about? How could this even happen?

After some time in deep introspection, out of this extremely remorseful event, one thing did become very clear for me, and that was the distinct impression that what I was looking at was just the twisted container that became her prison, keeping her from being physically liberated and free to fully engage in the world around her. I had this deep sense of knowing that everything that made my niece real to us, that created the fond memories, the love, and the connection we felt to her, was not in that container any more. I was

was looking at a shell of what she really was and what she meant to us during her time on this physical plane.

What we connected with was not the shell of my niece with all its various imperfections; what we were really connected with was her spirit, her soul, which I realized was immortal and free of the physical restrictions that had caused her so much pain throughout her life. I developed this sense of peace and comfort despite the corporeal reality that my niece was no longer with us.

Here is what became clear to me: as it is with any living organism, we experience life in two forms—the physical portion of our reality and the spiritual or soul version as well. Because we exist on the physical plane, and because of our conditioning and cultural beliefs, it's often easier to make sense of our lives on the physical level, so we tend to live to the limits of our five senses. We start to take as gospel that what we see, hear, smell, taste, and touch is the only reality that exists. What we haven't taken stock of is that within our hearts and minds, we work on a whole other level of living and experiencing. We live two lives: one in the physical world and the other in the spiritual reality. In my opinion, we spend about 80 percent of our time in the latter but only acknowledge and perceive 20 percent or less of it. Every time you wander off in deep thought and fantasy, you disassociate from your physical body to a world that you can paint to be either fearful or stupendous; this all depends on what experience you choose to create from your reality.

Here is the other lesson from this moment: between our internal and external lives, there is a bridge that helps to create the connection and make the physical life possible, and the thing that forms that bridge, I've discovered, is our breath. Breathing is linked to the initiation of life as well as the cessation of life. Babies are declared as arriving into life when they take their first breath, and human beings are declared as deceased when they expel their final breath. In between all this is a constant repetition of cycles of breathing, and the quality of those cycles is what really makes life possible.

I realized that when I felt the energy and the fluctuation in the body's tissues, what I was feeling was the breath of life that animates them. When I viewed the container that once belonged to my niece, I had a sense that it was just the shell and what was missing was that constant retraction and expansion that means life is at work. No wonder in meditation there is a strong emphasis on the breath; have you ever noticed that when you wander off in deep thought, sometimes the only thing that connects you back to the physical plane is the awareness that you've stopped breathing fully? When you bring your attention back to the physical reality, it's usually spurred on by this sudden need to take a deep and cleansing breath. Everything in life and every process that supports life goes through a cycle of respiration; it truly is the connector between our inner world of the spirit and soul and the outer world of our physical reality.

Let's summarize all of this information. My niece's passing made me enter into deep introspection and contemplation of life itself. What I realized is that our body is simply a vehicle, or a repository, for a much deeper world of experiences. When we look at someone, what we're really seeing is just the tip of the iceberg, and our senses perform a Gestalt by filling in the gaps between what we see and what we want to believe is the truth. The problem is that we often stay on a superficial level of understanding because our busy lifestyles and the hectic pace of today's society distract us, preventing us from expanding and fine-tuning our senses, so we are unable to read deeper and build our intuitions. In this state, we are prevented from building deeper and more refined levels of communication with each other.

Experience Number Four

As I continued on my path to the discovery of the spiritual essence, I began to take an even broader view of life and our roles in it. I am a big believer in a phrase I once heard from one of the most influential modern-day philosophers and teachers, author and speaker Jim Rohn. He passed away just a few years ago, but what an impact he made. He said, "Don't just get through your life; get from your life." When I heard that, it hit me that most of us just do what we can to get through life, and, when we take this kind of approach, we end up missing out on so many magical moments along the way because we get numb from the neck up in our quest to just make it through each day. Take, for instance, my next experience; this one really was the glue that stuck together most of my past experiences of the spiritual nature of our world.

Question: When was the last time you took a look around you to notice the environment and the many activities that go on every day to create the beauty that we have as the background to our daily experiences? I'm not talking about spending hours and hours outside taking in nature, although that would be amazing; I mean to just stop, use all your senses for a while, and take in the surroundings while you drive or walk to work or school. It literally takes nothing to shift away from your electronic device or from your internal worries about the past or future to take notice of what's going on around you. Then, you will get a true appreciation of the magic that goes on in the background of our days amidst the self-imposed stresses and disconnection we often experience on a daily basis.

Many years ago, I decided to take my own advice to become mindful of paying attention to the so-called "little things" around me. The first thing I did was to take notice of this particular plant that would every so often catch my eye, yet I never stopped to give it enough time and attention. In the front of my home are hostas, which are known for their automated annual return and their timely response to the change in seasons. Each year at spring, as the snow begins to melt away, as I leave the house, I watch the hostas bud and gradually blossom into their final summer bloom. By about July, what was once a one-inch-diameter patch of green bud just poking through the ground is now a flourishing garden of flora and fauna, taking up the entire garden. This got me thinking about the innate intelligence of nature and how it effortlessly and consistently performs these small and inconspicuous acts of brilliance and beauty. My next thought was to wonder, *What is this intelligence that gives the plants and animals the blueprint to guide their automated patterns?*

After some introspection, meditation, and journaling, I began to realize that this seemingly simple and effortless process is a reflection of nature's spiritual essence. What we miss every day, if we allow ourselves to go to sleep on our journeys through life, is the fundamental process of nature expressing itself through the environment. There are so many instances of such great innate intelligence in nature that it boggles the mind. Nature follows, without effort, its predetermined design and blueprint. Nature does not get in its own way when expressing itself; only humans do. Through our habitual lifestyle choices, our eating patterns, and our increasing stress loads, we are constantly interrupting the natural flow and processing of our perfectly designed blueprint, making it that much more difficult to connect with our own spiritual essences.

If we extend this thought just a little further to the process of conception, over approximately forty weeks, if all goes as planned, human beings are capable of creating a new life. In this process, the fetus follows a predetermined design, each day following a precise process of creation. When you step back and consider what has to happen in that forty-week period of time, it will vex your mind and return you to the awe-inspiring wisdom of nature. So what's behind that process? The best minds have never been able to completely figure it out. All we can do is to step back and respect the timing of the process and just accept what is. Once again, I think the game was set up so we will never be able to fully figure things out. If we did, we would find a way to manipulate the magic and become even less appreciative of the process.

Greatness Journey: Four Steps to Rebuilding and Enhancing Your Spiritual Essence

Information is just that, information. So how do we put it all into use? How do we once again restore and rejuvenate our spiritual essences? I was like most people in society today; I was on my path with my head down, checking off my to-do list, and becoming more and more disconnected from my spiritual essence. Most of my clients who seek help in bringing back balance and some semblance of sanity in their lives admit that they spend so much time either in the past, with feelings of regret and resentment, or in the future, worrying about anxiety and stress, that they find it extremely difficult to be in the present moments of their lives.

Over the years, and by way of helping hundreds of clients to reconnect with their spiritual essences, I have developed four particular methods of reconnection to the magic show going on around us. These are four simple but powerful steps that you can implement right now in order to regain control and feel a sense of empowerment over your world.

Step 1: Remember to Breathe

This seems so simple, but I have found that this is a lost art in our society. When we stress and worry, we often become disconnected and distant from our present moments. One thing you will notice is that you will often catch yourself wandering off, deep in thought and playing the scary movies of your reality in the theater of the mind. The only times you realize that you're not even in the here and now are typically when you catch yourself in need of a full, deep, cleansing breath. This is a signal that nature itself is taking over, and it forces you to follow the naturally designed blueprint.

When we breathe, the myriad of processes that are linked to this simple act cannot be measured. Your diaphragm, the large sheet of muscle and membrane that separates the contents of your ribcage and your abdomen and is the key structure in the mechanics of breathing, traverses some of the major vessels within your body; your heart and lungs, your digestive system, liver and kidneys, as well as an efficient flow of blood and body fluids are all in direct relationship to an efficient and fully functioning diaphragm. Due to our modern-day lifestyles and postural habits, we are often guilty of allowing ourselves to lose the ability to maintain an efficient use of our diaphragms. We typically end up breathing from our chests, leading to short and inefficient movement of the diaphragm, which doesn't lend to efficient overall functioning of the body's capacity to restore and energize itself.

Here are some simple steps:

1. Set yourself a reminder about every fifteen minutes or
    so, either on your computer or your smartphone, to
    take deep and purposeful breaths throughout your day.

2. You want to simply and easily remind yourself to breathe in through the nose and out through pursed lips to a count of four, with one-second intervals between each breath. Your best bet is to make sure that each breath causes your stomach to rise and fall, signaling efficient movement of your diaphragm.

3. With each breath, you will begin to have a sense of clarity and reconnection to your body and the present moment. It would be very difficult to take a deep and purposeful breath without becoming reconnected to and present in your day.

Step 2: Remove You from the Equation: Don't Take Life Personally

This is another amazing way to stay connected to your spiritual essence—remove your ego from the experience, and stop taking life and yourself so seriously. Nothing separates you from your spiritual essence faster than going through your day taking everything personally. When we continue to make every experience personal attacks on our egos, we move into the emotions of resentment, shame, guilt, and anger. These emotions prevent us from reaching and maintaining blissful states by coloring simple and meaningless events as personal attacks on our egos, and when the ego feels as if it has been attacked, then all the gloves are off and there are no holds barred.

Here's your solution: separate fact from fiction. Fact: the car in front of you did cut you off or does drive slowly; fiction: that driver is out on a personal vendetta against you and only you! He or she is doing everything to completely throw you off your game and just seems to be going everywhere you are going and purpose-fully driving you crazy! Fact: your funds are low this month and you may have to scrape to find enough money to cover the basics; fiction: you are a failure and you have always struggled with money. You can never get ahead. The money belongs in the hands of the one-percenters, and all the small folks will always be behind the eight ball! It must be your lot in life to struggle. Life is just too hard, and you can never have enough money because the world is set up against you.

I once overheard the owner of the business beside me abso-lutely losing his mind because he had an assumption that someone in the next unit was laughing at him. He banged on the walls and shouted profanity and threats, only to find out that our neighbor was just a happy person and laughing was what she did by nature. In his moment of anger and worry about the present status of his business, he completely distorted his reality, causing him to lash out in anger. If he had been able to practice separating fact from fiction, he would have saved himself a whole world of stress and embarrassment.

Step 3: Meditate: Listen to Your Inner Voice

Start listening to your inner voice and paying attention to those "gut" feelings you get every so often. How many times have you been so consumed with your situation that you became over-whelmed and defeated by it? When you're in this position, it's very difficult to find solutions to your problems. As previously cited, Al-bert Einstein said, "We can't solve problems by using the same kind of thinking we used when we created them." Regular meditation helps you to tune into your inner voice and remove yourself from your current situation. You will become the watcher in your movie, which gives you a chance to take an objective viewpoint of your situation, removing the subjective and emotional vantage point that causes you to become irrational.

Step 4: Stop and Smell the Roses: Practice Gratitude

Stop and smell the roses. Heard this before? Well, have you done it? I have personally coached so many people who have managed to achieve a great level of success toward their desired goals, yet when I ask about their feelings around their accomplishments, I am surprised to find that they remain in states of sadness with relentless needs to feel like they are enough. On further questioning, it's even more interesting that this state of being enough is never really defined and always moving. These people have never given themselves a chance to stop and smell the roses so they can appreciate their journeys. This relentless wanting moves them into mindsets of lack and limitation. This kind of state nudges you out of the sense of gratitude, which is the entryway to your spiritual essence. Regularly practicing gratitude is the key to feeling at peace within yourself and opening up to all the goodness that the universe has to offer. When you practice envy and relentless wanting, you fail to see and take advantage of the many opportunities that life has to offer.

Afterword

Achieving greatness or staying in mediocrity does not reflect a judgment statement about a person's character; instead, it reveals the strategy someone is using to run his or her life. If you find that where you are now is not where you want to be or planned on being, then the exercise for you is to step back and look at the strategy you're using in any given situation. If your strategy is leading to a life of happiness and fulfillment on your terms, then you're living out your greatness. If the way in which you're living brings you to continuous stress and frustration, then you're using strategies and processes that are in the category of the mediocre.

No matter where you are now or whatever your past story was, you can turn it all around by adopting the mediocrity-to-greatness process. The magic of being human is that we are not genetically wired to follow one script. We have the abilities to completely change our course in a second. All it takes is a decision to do just that. Where you start has no determining factor for where you will finally end up. I am a testament to that fact, and this book is the proof.

I can remember a time not too far back when I could not string together a full paragraph that wasn't filled with grammatical errors and typos. Not to mention the fact that I would be booted out of any academic establishment for blatant and outright plagiarism due to the fact that I had no clue as to the gravity of such an act. That, you could say, was a mediocrity mindset. Why would I admit that and not just claim to be ignorant and blame it on lack of education? I could play that card to relieve myself of ownership. However, the blame game is a weak stand to take and lacks the power to facilitate the change we need to move toward our personal greatness.

I say that I was using a strategy of mediocrity because I could've chosen to go the extra mile and educate myself by improving my writing skills. Instead, I chose to stay the same, wishing things would change for me instead of creating the change I wanted. Greatness is about attacking life from a proactive stance, while being mediocre is all about living life passively in hopes that all will turn out the way you want it. During the first years of my life, I can easily say that most of my strategies were from a mindset of mediocrity—medio-cre thinking, eating, and earning power. When I decided to adopt a greatness mindset and started to apply myself, everything turned around for me. I moved from being passive to being 100 percent active in turning my life around. From that day of decision to the present day, everything has turned to my favor: better relationships, better finances, better health, better mental and emotional balance, and an improved spiritual connection and balance.

The mediocrity mindset is insidious and infectious. It can spread and propagate itself into your six essences. Before you know it, you're living how you don't want to live, acting how you don't want to act, and facing a reality you never imagined because you wanted so much more when your passion for life was at its summit! Then, a few unfortunate incidences and a streak of life's inevitable learning moments occur, and you unconsciously slip into the trap of consistently thinking thoughts of mediocrity. You find yourself looking at the negative side of life, and you begin to expect the worst, even when things are at their best. You begin to take on the mindset that if things are going well, something is bound to happen sooner rather than later, so you better delay your happiness in order to buffer the incoming "bad times" that always, in your opinion, follow the good.

There is a noticeable phenomenon that occurs with these two contrasting mindsets. First, the mediocrity mindset is passive, powerful, insidious, and fast acting, and it has the ability to become intractable. It requires no effort to implement in your mind, body, and soul. When it becomes a part of your entire being, it wreaks havoc and can paralyze you with fear, doubt, and pessimism. On the other hand, the greatness mindset is equally powerful, but it takes active and conscious programming to see the benefits. At the beginning of the journey of implementation, it's often a very weak bond and can be broken at any provocation or reminder of the mediocrity mindset. This is why those who achieve the greatness mindset typically build a level of preeminence and notoriety that often leads them to the status of legendary. This also explains why the percentage of people who achieve this status is very small and will probably remain that way for all time. Moving from mediocrity to greatness is all about having clarity, taking action, and being focused on the life you want. This is the barrier to entry that seems to stop most people dead in their tracks!

It's an amazing irony that as much as some of us detest with passion our present statuses in life, we tend not to want to change the familiar. A couple of thoughts come to mind—first, human beings have an affinity for certainty in life. A number of psychologists have said that it is a human need that we strive to fulfill at any cost.

Even when our situation is at its most dire, having a sense of certainty keeps us wrapped up in its clutches due to this need. Second, the pain of our present circumstances often isn't strong enough to make change happen. The status quo is comfortable and familiar, and it requires no effort to stay in the comfort zone. The combination of these two traits keeps us debilitated and stuck on all levels—mind, body, and soul.

The mediocrity mindset can happen to the best of us, and it's a state of being that can be unrelenting, even when you have achieved some of your biggest and loftiest goals. This reminds me of the quote that says, "Nothing fails like success," because it's when people are most successful that some get fooled into becoming complacent and forgetting about what got them there in the first place. Actually, the mediocrity mindset can rear its ugly head at any time during our evolution toward our highest and best selves. Since human beings are limitless in their potential, constant evolution is our birthright, which explains why those achievers in life who seem to live out the greatness mindset are always looking for the next opportunity to grow and serve. In this mindset, there is a strong and inherent need to flower and become more of who you are each and every day.

So how do you know when you're living under the control of the mediocrity mindset? Here are a few indications:

- Friends and family consistently comment that they see more in you than you see in yourself, but you're unable to make the change you need due to fear and doubt.

- You have an unrelenting desire to be, do, and have more than your present level in life, but you pass up each opportunity to grow by making excuses as to why it can't be done.

- You have a strong need to serve the greater good, but the fear of becoming vulnerable to criticism makes you frozen.

- You have an amazing ability to see and feel the needs of others and how to meet them, but you can think of every reason why you can't get started.

- External events have a profound effect on your mind and emotions and leave you paralyzed.

- You move to a competitive and pessimistic mindset when others mention taking actions on their dreams.

- You habitually retreat into safety when faced with a chance to grow into the next level of your greatness.

- You believe, and often voice, that the world is set up against you and the odds are not in your favor.

- You blame your race, gender, social status, upbringing, co-workers, friends, or some past event for your inability to move toward your greatness.

- You are often overwhelmed by your situation and cannot identify a solution to find your way out.

These are just a few of the situations that will often indicate that you are living under the strong powers of the mediocrity mindset. If you've checked one or more of these points, then my guess is that you are experiencing a great deal of self-induced fear and frustration about your situation.

On the other side of the spectrum, here are some keys to let you know that you are living on the edge of greatness, and with just one tweak of your process you will be playing your biggest game:

- You are not afraid to take calculated actions to bring your dreams to fruition.

- Your mind consistently thinks on solutions, and you know that there are many different ways to solve any problem or remove any roadblock.

- You are constantly searching for ways to improve and grow.

- You are a master of time, and you realize the value of an hour.

- You are a master of money, and you realize the potential power to convert time into money and money into serving the greater good.

- You realize the value of the "slight edge" principle, in which it takes only small steps in the right direction to make massive differences.

- You know that the journey of a thousand miles begins with the first step, so you are never overwhelmed by the entire journey.

- You know the value of networking and the idea that there are only six degrees or less of separation between you and the people of resources you need to turn it all around.

- Your habitual mindset is not fixed on what can't be done but on how to get it done.

- You are resilient, and you face your fear, knowing that it becomes the foundation of your new strength.

These are just some of the indications that you are equipped with the tools you need to aggressively go after your greatness. If you have found that you are deficient in one or more of the traits on our list, then you now have the beginning steps to taking action for change.

Getting into the "greatness zone" is possible, but staying there is the real trick. With constant outside influences always pushing us off course, we must be mindful of frequently taking inventory of our present state of thinking and behaving. As the saying goes, "What gets measured will usually improve." In order to consistently remain in the greatness zone, I want you to think about any action that makes you feel less than your greatest self; then I want you to assess whether or not you are living out of your greatness paradigm. This can apply to your thoughts, emotions, finances, diet and life-style, and your physical body. The brain will answer whatever question you ask of it, so routinely assessing yourself to ensure you're on track to your greatness is the key to changing for the better.

The life you want is waiting for you. It literally will take you only a second to make that change; you just have to decide that you want it, and you will take the necessary steps to change. We all have only twenty-four hours per day, and what we do with those hours is the most important task we should attend to. An hour lost is lost forever; we can never get it back. My advice is to treat time as if it is your greatest and most valuable asset, because it is. Those who are truly successful and who live to express their greatness know the value of time and use it wisely, each and every day. Success leaves clues, and I think it's wise that we follow these clues.

In order to discover your greatness, you must focus on reigniting your passions by finding your authenticity, setting big goals, managing your time, managing your money, developing a blueprint program to increase your physical health, managing and improving your personal and professional relationships, and learning how to take consistent and massive action! That is the ultimate goal of the mediocrity-to-greatness process, to live life on your terms and to discover what enlivens you and facilitates your greatness.

You will find a Mediocrity2Greatness assessment form in Appendix B of this book. See how you rate in your life because what gets measured will improve.

Appendix A:
List of Values

Instructions: From the list below, first pick 25 values that most resonate with you. Second, narrow those 25 picks down to your top 10 choices that most describe your values. Third, narrow your choices down to your top 5 most treasured values; last, let's get to #1!

This is the value that drives almost every decision you make, both consciously and unconsciously.

1. Abundance	17. Dependability	33. Health
2. Acceptance	18. Desire	34. Honesty
3. Ambition	19. Determination	35. Integrity
4. Appreciation	20. Discipline	36. Leadership
5. Balance	21. Economy	37. Love
6. Bravery	22. Encouragement	38. Peace
7. Capability	23. Fairness	39. Passion
8. Care	24. Faith	40. Power
9. Commitment	25. Family	41. Respect
10. Compassion	26. Fidelity	42. Service
11. Connection	27. Fitness	43. Sincerity
12. Contribution	28. Freedom	44. Trust
13. Cooperation	29. Fun	45. Unity
14. Creativity	30. Generosity	46. Variety
15. Credibility	31. Gratitude	47. Vitality
16. Decisiveness	32. Growth	48. Wisdom

Appendix B:
Assessment Description and Form

Emotional Essence; shame, guilt, resentment, fear, and the like are all destructive emotions that many in our society struggle with each day. Ridding yourself of these emotions is a major key to getting to the next level of peak performance.

Mental Essence; this has to do with your ability to maintain a stable mental focus throughout your day. The biggest roadblock to attaining peak performance is not having clarity and definiteness of purpose. How will you ever get what you want if you can't even articulate it yourself? You must work diligently to attain a clear vision of exactly what you want, in order to get what you need.

Physical Essence; all your dreams and desires would be nothing without your health. It's amazing that physical health falls down on our list of importance when it comes to reaching our goals. Wouldn't it be a shame to get to your goal and not be able to fully enjoy the fruits of your labour because you don't have optimal health.

Chemical Essence; with respect to peak performance, food should be thought of as its chemical components and how it interacts with your body to produce a certain output. Try to keep the *emotional* aspect of food out of food, because when eating is an emotional response, this is when it becomes a losing battle in your health and wellness formula.

Material Essence; this has to do with your relationship with your material world. So many times it has been said that money is the root of all evil. So much so, that achieving financial success has become a taboo subject that most people feel ashamed about honouring themselves by getting what they want on a material level.

Spiritual Essence; simply put, being spiritual is simply getting connected with something higher than yourself. Being spiritual is realizing that you're simply a very small cog in the wheel of life. When you step back and look to the forces that govern nature, you realize that you are indeed a miracle of creation, and to tap into that brilliance is just one route to achieving peak performance.

6 Essences Assessment Scale

"It's been said that what you monitor gets better, and energy flows where attention goes." At this time, let's step back and get a baseline of your current status in order to see where you need to put most of your focus so you can achieve levels of peak performance.

Place a mark on each scale to show your *current* perceived state of your levels of balance.

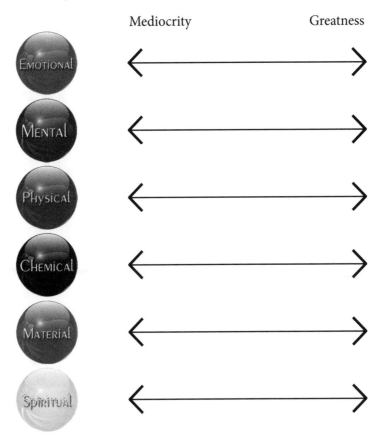

About the Author

A lvin Brown is the owner and creator of a very successful multidisciplinary health, wellness, and peak performance center located in Ontario, Canada. He has dedicated himself to creating a team of professionals with the aim of helping their clients achieve optimal health and life balance—mind, body, and soul. Born in Kingston, Jamaica, to a single mother of five, Alvin has risen from abject poverty, violence, homelessness, an alcoholic father, and broken relationships by applying the life principles laid out in this book. He married his high school sweetheart, had four amazing and successful kids, and eventually became a successful entrepreneur, performance consultant, international speaker, and now author.

Alvin has spent the past three decades in relentless pursuit of personal greatness. This quest began in the field of sports, achieving recognition in collegiate wrestling and professional Tae Kwon Do competitions. He also spent time as a professional dancer and as an amateur boxer. This same pursuit for greatness extended into his professional life and his studies in osteopathic manual practice, registered massage therapy, energy medicine, natural nutrition, acupuncture, and Chinese medicine. Alvin earned his undergraduate degree in psychology from Trent University, located in Peterborough, Ontario, and his manual osteopathic diploma from the British School of Osteopathic Medicine.